Praise

"A powerful playbook on now to stay close to the changing consumer in our fast-paced world and turn the consumer insights function into a competitive advantage for your business. A great read for marketing and consumer insights leaders alike."
— **Ravi Dhar, Director**, Yale Center for Customer Insights and Professor of Marketing and Psychology, Yale School of Management

"Data really is the new oil; *The Consumer Insights Revolution* is the guidebook on how to build a modern refinery to deliver real, tangible impact from it. It's indispensable and inspiring!"
— **Leonard F. Murphy**, Chief Advisor for Insights and Development, Greenbook

"People, processes, and technology are the foundation of modern business transformation. In *The Consumer Insights Revolution*, the authors reveal powerful lessons on leveraging technology partnerships to elevate a global brand's consumer focus. Packed with actionable insights and forward-looking strategies, this book empowers marketing and insights professionals to drive

impactful change and build greater influence within their organizations."
— **George Kadifa**, Managing Director, Sumeru Equity Partners

"From agile methodologies to AI integration, *The Consumer Insights Revolution* offers a goldmine of nuggets for anyone navigating the future of Market Research. Written by four of the most innovative icons in the industry, this book is a must-read."
— **Michelle Gansle**, Chief Data & Analytics Officer, McDonald's

"A thought-provoking and necessary read for the market research industry; this book encourages market researchers to push the boundaries to innovate and influence in their careers."
— **Lauren Governale**, Senior Director, Head of Customer Insights & UX research, Hims & Hers

"Energizing and a must read for researchers and human intelligence experts who want to push the boundaries of what is possible to ensure that the Insights ecosystem thrives. Some great inspiration on how organizations can shift from knowledge management to decision management, ensuring that Insights teams step into the role of strategic partner vs just research generator. Love love love!"
— **Nic Umana**, Global Agile Innovation Human Intelligence Director, Mars

The

Consumer Insights Revolution

**Transforming market research
for competitive advantage**

**Steve
Phillips**

**Ryan
Barry**

**Stephan
Gans**

**Kate
Schardt**

R^ethink

First published in Great Britain in 2024
by Rethink Press (www.rethinkpress.com)

Contents

Foreword

PepsiCo's mission is to create billions of smiles, shape the future of our categories, and accelerate our growth, while making a positive impact on people and planet. In this journey, the PepsiCo Consumer organization, which I have the privilege to lead, has a distinctive contribution to make.

The truth is that creating products and building brands that resonate with people is hard work. Marketers, innovators, and designers meet this challenge head-on every day with an insatiable appetite to push the envelope and create work that moves the meter for their consumers and brands. However, effective work isn't just the most aesthetically pleasing ad or the loudest new product on the shelves; rather, it starts with the ability to connect brands to the lives and needs of consumers in a way that is relevant and authentic.

In this complex environment, the role of our Consumer Insights and Analytics function is more important than ever as we strive to anticipate the rapidly changing needs of the people we serve. I am impressed with PepsiCo's ongoing multi-year journey led by Stephan Gans, PepsiCo's Chief Consumer Insights Officer, who, together with his Insights Leadership Team, is transforming our many separate insights departments into one aligned global function that leverages its scale to build competitive advantage for the company.

For PepsiCo, the key to leveraging our scale in consumer insights lies in digitalization of our key tools, and providing access to data for all our teams around the world. Kate Schardt, the PepsiCo head of Global Insights Capabilities and Partnerships, has embarked on a bold mission and partnered with Zappi to create Ada. *So what is Ada?* Ada is our own insights operating system where PepsiCo employees around the globe can tap into a lifetime of shared knowledge and learn. Ada has become the human-centric heartbeat of our marketing strategy, providing a shared space to test new and exciting ideas, connect data from pretesting all the way through purchase, and look deeper into what drives our consumers' behavior.

Through our partnership with Zappi, PepsiCo has been able to not only rally around a standardized way to evaluate marketing ideas and execution but also to raise the bar on what constitutes great creative execution and innovation by linking the consumer performance indicators to PepsiCo's proprietary return on investment (ROI) engine. Also, because the benchmarking we use is not a "black box," we curate the standards we're setting for these comparisons ourselves. While Ada allows us to take work in-house where we own the interpretation and action of our insights, this means we can develop local talent along with our insights experts to work with greater speed and make smarter decisions.

But we've discovered an even more critical benefit: Ada enables company-wide learning. Indeed, everyone can have access to all data anytime. This means each time one market tests a new idea, the whole company can learn from the results and become smarter. This is how our scale becomes an advantage, and how we make increasingly better consumer-centric commercial decisions at all levels, especially at the market level.

Zappi has been one of our main technology partners from the start of Ada, working with us in lockstep to create tools built around our priority needs. Without the partnership with Zappi, our vision would have taken five or ten years longer to come to fruition. While at a glance a large multinational company partnering with a technology startup may seem like an unlikely match, Zappi provided an access point to new technology, as well as an infectious energy and ambition to drive change not only in PepsiCo but in the consumer insights industry. We are grateful for the partnership and vision of fellow authors Steve Phillips and Ryan Barry, for challenging the status quo and bringing a bias for action to our work each day.

Stephan and Kate will be the first to tell you that it isn't always easy getting to a point where a global company of PepsiCo's scale harnesses insights as instrumental to our day-to-day jobs. It requires an ongoing and concerted effort to change hearts and minds. In the pages that follow, you will discover the process through which PepsiCo Insights is making a real impact on the organization thanks to the resilience and ambition of the insights leadership and their Zappi partnership. In addition, as with the fast-moving nature of both consumers and technology, this book will also give you a flavor of the next evolution of consumer insights, and why artificial intelligence (AI) could and will change everything.

I hope that as you read about our story, you can draw parallels with your own experiences and find inspiration to grow yourself, your team, and your organization into more human-centric ways of working. We are on a journey too and would welcome your ideas and builds.

Happy reading,

Jane

Jane Wakely, Executive Vice President at PepsiCo, Chief Consumer and Marketing Officer, and Chief Growth Officer for PepsiCo's International Foods business

Introduction

It was June 2017 when Stephan Gans joined PepsiCo as Chief Consumer Insights and Analytics Officer. He knew that his function was facing a huge challenge. The company's leadership had lost faith in the insights function's ability to drive competitive advantage and told him that his main objective was to slash costs. If he didn't find a way to prove and improve the value of the work he and his colleagues did, they would be in trouble.

The first thing he set out to do was to talk with the many insights teams stationed around the world in the company's business territories. Luckily for him, he found a diverse range of bright, hard-working, and experienced market research professionals. They all told him the same things: The tools from their incumbent vendors were outdated, everything took too long, and it all cost too much. The slowness in particular was a problem—it took weeks to get a piece of research back—and this caused friction between insights teams and their marketing colleagues.

Not only that, but there was little joined-up thinking, both within PepsiCo and among its vendors. The insights teams were doing great work, but there was virtually no leverage of best practice, talent exchange, or information-sharing between them. When Stephan asked the Mexico team what was going on in Mexico, they had lots of information to share, but they had no straightforward way to discover what the equivalent team in Germany knew. What happened in Mexico stayed in Mexico, and what happened in Germany stayed in Germany. Stephan called this problem "local for local." While marketing was increasingly starting to think and work globally, market research was limited to its own country or region.

Ironically, one of the only things that united Stephan's market research teams, apart from a limited number of common tools, were the agencies they worked with. Even there, the unifying effect was small. As is standard for large research organizations, vendors were set up to mirror PepsiCo's global structure, with offices in each of the territories and markets the company served. They too bypassed the global in favor of the local, which, for a multinational such as

PepsiCo, took away a significant part of its potential competitive advantage.

The fact that consumer insights teams were effectively living on their own individual islands, doing their own thing, their own way, also denied PepsiCo the opportunity to learn and grow from the data that they already had. When Stephan asked one of his vendors why they couldn't share information between their own branches more easily, the vendor said, "It's funny you should ask that, because I have a report here you might be interested in." It consisted of four pages crammed with tiny print, listing all the research projects commissioned by PepsiCo for the past four months on the breakfast opportunity for Quaker Oats in thirty-five different markets, for millions of dollars. Yet nobody had shared these projects with anyone else to find commonalities or aligning methodologies. When Stephan multiplied this report by the number of brands the business had, it was clearly madness.

Stephan realized that his consumer insights people had become order takers for market research projects, a bit like clerks behind a post office counter. When a marketer needed research, they approached the counter and briefed the consumer insights person, who gave them a price and an estimated timescale for the job. The "clerk" didn't question the marketer about what was in the package, whether there was a better option that the marketer didn't know about, or even if it needed to be sent at all.

Given that PepsiCo was spending hundreds of millions of dollars per year on consumer insights and was determined to become—like all businesses—more consumer centric, it was clear that drastic change was required. The insights managers needed to transform from order takers into indispensable business partners.

Stephan began by developing an inspiring but simple vision for the market research function and starting to articulate what it would take to drive the transformation. He also initiated the process of uniting the market research islands into one nation by creating what he called the Global Insights Council (GIC). GIC was a group of fifteen insights leaders representing PepsiCo's business regions, as well as its central and global capabilities. He discovered that these leaders shared a powerful desire to become more impactful. While they'd long recognized some of the issues that Stephan had uncovered, their isolation had made it difficult to address them. They were eager to work more closely with one another to develop an integrated, global approach. For that to happen, they agreed on two goals: that PepsiCo should become the owner of its consumer data and insights, and that this ownership should be a cornerstone of its future competitive advantage.

Those were their goals, but the "how" of these changes meant that the consumer insights teams could no longer afford to work in a sequential way, as clerks taking orders and delivering results. Marketing had become a real-time game, necessitating tools that supported agile decision making. Since the consumer insights function also needed the meta-learning that would come from owning consumer data and sharing it among themselves, they could no longer outsource it to traditional market research agencies. Consumer insights required their own digital platform that could be accessed by anyone around the business who had a need for data. They couldn't achieve this transformation alone, so they looked for a partner who was digitally based, set up to work globally, and eager to challenge the status quo.

Stephan and the GIC chose Zappi as that partner because it was the most advanced digital market research platform provider around. Together, the two companies embarked on a venture that's unique in the consumer packaged goods industry. They committed to surfing the wave of digital consumer insights as a joint endeavor, learning from each other and growing as they went along. In the process, Zappi worked closely with a small group of PepsiCo Insights talent to create world-class tools that exponentially improved PepsiCo's marketing effectiveness.

The responsibility now rested on Stephan and the GIC. They had to prove to themselves—and to the rest of PepsiCo—that creating a digital platform that brought their data together for sharing and creating insights across the global brand would make the whole business more consumer focused. They weren't disappointed. Five years after making this change, PepsiCo's creative effectiveness has improved by almost one-third across all its advertising. This equated to the business gaining hundreds of millions of dollars in value in just one year. To date, the platform has generated over 6,000 research projects (delivered five times faster than before) and over $100 million in savings and improvements. Stephan and the GIC have built a culture of agility, speed, and efficiency that has led to the business's recognition as an industry leader in consumer insights. Rather than being slashed, Stephan's budget has grown.

What about you?

In the rest of this book, you'll learn more about how PepsiCo's consumer insights professionals evolved from order takers to business partners and the amazing benefits this has continued to bring to the organization. For now, though, let's pause and take a moment to reflect on your situation. Do any of the challenges we've discussed sound familiar to you? Perhaps you've experienced feeling isolated from what's going on in the rest of your company. Maybe you've grown frustrated with the sluggish pace and silos in your market research projects. It's possible that you feel undervalued, seen as an "order taker" rather than as a professional who can shape your company's direction through your skills and expertise.

Yet, shouldn't it be a great time to work in market research? CEOs around the world say that they want their businesses to be more consumer centric. Of course they do. Without a growing and profitable consumer base, their company has no future. The abilities to understand consumer behavior, create products or services aligned with predictions, and successfully market them are foundational. We're guessing that you chose your field because you're interested in consumers and what makes them tick: why they do what they do, buy what they buy, and think what they think. If consumer centricity rules, then the need to provide great insights to support business decisions is at an all-time high. By rights, you're the most important department in your organization, so why doesn't it feel like that?

There are several reasons, the main one being that you're trying to make the business more consumer focused while dealing with fast turnaround times in marketing and product development. You have a conflict between the need to explore consumer preferences in depth and the requirement to do it in a way that doesn't hold up progress. That's not your fault; it's a product of the tools you're using, which prevent you from innovating. Traditional, full-service agencies are cumbersome and slow, and while a range of new providers have recently evolved to speed things up, they've also complicated the landscape. Where once there were only full-service companies, qualitative specialists, and panels, now there are also end-to-end platforms, DIY platforms, consultancies, knowledge management companies, specialist customer or user experience agencies, qualitative agencies, and specialist methodology vendors. The list goes on.

This complexity makes it tough to be a consumer insights professional. It also doesn't help that the framework used by many corporate insights departments is no longer fit for purpose, as it comes from a pre-digital, pre-agile age. You can choose a shiny new vendor with a buzzword-heavy solution such as AI, machine learning, natural language processing, automation, or "always-on," but you can't make progress by adding a buzzword on top of a broken model.

If "broken" seems extreme to you, please hear us out. Having spent our combined careers working both with and within market research departments across all industries and geographies, we watch the following challenges play out all the time. See if they sound familiar.

- **Rubber stamping:** Consumer insights teams often work in silos, with marketing, sales, and other areas of the business viewing them not as part of the team—or even as an insights center of excellence—but as separate and disconnected. Too often, insights is an afterthought, called in only to green-light a decision that's already been made, to tick a box to get through a gateway in development, or to validate content so the marketing person doesn't get fired. For this reason, insights professionals are viewed as "rubber stampers," not as consumer experts. Because they lack independence in many organizations, they're not inclined to bite the hand that feeds them, so they struggle to influence decision making.

- **Fire drills:** When the insights team sits in a silo and isn't considered until late in the process, every request is urgent. Often, the marketing and sales teams are similarly overwhelmed and don't have time for a proper briefing or to consider what they really want to know. If you're busy putting out imaginary fires, you don't have the time or budget to build a better process.

- **Decks, decks, decks:** How much of your time do you spend making decks? If you're not fixing vendor decks that have missed the mark (because you didn't have time to brief the vendor properly), then you're customizing insights decks for disparate internal stakeholders. There are better ways to use consumer insights to inspire your colleagues to be more creative and build your brand.

- **Faster? Cheaper? Better?:** There are many more types of market research vendors than before, and salespeople are competing for your attention. Not only does this take up your valuable time with emails, cold calls, and content to read but, when you do agree to take a pitch, you find that everyone is promising the holy trinity: faster, cheaper, and better. How can you decipher where the value is? Who should you work with? How can you build a roster of trusted advisers?

- **Juggling politics:** You want to develop more effective ads iteratively with consumers, but because some of the metrics are linked to remuneration in the marketing team, you can't. Your CEO has a pet project that you end up wasting time on, even though you already know that your customers will hate it, because you don't have the specific market research data that will convince them to put it to rest. All organizations are political, but politics shouldn't be your job.

- **Juggling projects:** Your work is project-based, and while you learn from each individual project, there's no way to tie your insights together. Each time there's a requirement, you need to set up a new project, so you're always busy writing briefs and choosing between vendors. That only leaves you time to innovate tactically around the edges rather than to drive change in your company. If you'd wanted to be a project manager you'd have gone into project management, not market research.

The upshot is that, while everyone is talking about the need to be consumer centric, all the above factors get in the way of achieving it. Let's face it, the consequences of not being consumer focused can be dire. Look no further than Quibi. The streaming service, founded in 2018, raised an enormous $1.75 billion in funding ahead of its launch in April 2020. Eight months later, Quibi had shut down, its content library sold to Roku for a mere $100 million.[1] One of the reasons is that its paid, mobile-only offering wasn't in line with what consumers wanted and subscriber counts waned. The problem didn't lie with the streaming content but with the company's lack of understanding of its end users.

This situation leaves you trying to reach the promised land of consumer centricity without a definitive road map. The requests for more decks, more projects, and more meetings take up your working day and probably your evening too. Occasionally, you get to do the awesome work that you came into this role for: to find out what motivates people, for what occasions they buy your product, what else they're buying, and how they live and act in their homes. Most of the time, however, consumer insights is seen as an administrative function rather than a strategic pillar of the business. We're sorry to say it, but this means that, unless you change and innovate, you'll see your resources scaled back.

---

1   T Spangler, "Roku acquires global rights to 75-plus Quibi shows, will stream them for free", *Variety* (January 8, 2021), https://variety.com/2021/digital/news/roku-acquires-quibi-shows-free-streaming-1234881238, accessed May 29, 2024

Why listen to us?

We, your four authors, work for two separate businesses: Stephan Gans and Kate Schardt for PepsiCo, and Steve Phillips and Ryan Barry for digital market research platform Zappi. There are good reasons for us to team up to write this book. The main one is that we come from different backgrounds and experiences and therefore have different vantage points on the subject of market research. Despite that, we've come to the same valuable conclusions. Let's give you a brief overview of what each of us has to offer.

Stephan started his career in marketing at Unilever, which he left after fifteen years to help build a global marketing consultancy. After advising many leading brands there, he moved to branding consultancy firm Interbrand as Chief Strategy Officer. His current role at PepsiCo is his first consumer insights job, giving him the advantage of a fresh perspective and a deep understanding of what marketers need from insights professionals.

Kate is Vice President of Global Insights Capabilities and Partnerships at PepsiCo, with over twenty years of marketing, insights, and analytics experience. She has led the implementation of the company's digital consumer insights platform from the start, working alongside Zappi to make it a success. Her contribution to this book is invaluable, showing the reality of what it takes to transform a market research function.

Steve is the Chief Executive Officer and cofounder of Zappi and a specialist on behavioral economics. An innovative thinker who's passionate about how technology can automate and improve the market research process, he spends much of his time planning for the future. To him, staying constantly on the lookout for ways to evolve and grow should always be an integral part of market research so that it can empower creators with the data they need.

Ryan is President of Zappi and runs its operations, a role that has him spending a lot of time with Zappi's customers around the word. He helps consumer insights leaders and their teams to discover what they need their departments to deliver and supports them in achieving it. Having worked in the consumer data business for sixteen years, he's consulted with hundreds of brands and their insights departments. In that time, he's been inspired by the many innovative insights leaders and practitioners who are doing things differently, but he's also seen a lot who struggle to make an impact on their businesses and manage their workloads. It's his aim to put that right.

What you'll get from this book

Jeff Bezos, the founder of Amazon, was renowned for leaving an empty chair at the conference table to symbolize the company's customer. This gesture served as a constant reminder that consumer needs should always be included in decision making. This book shows that you can do even better than that by turning market research data into that empty chair. Whenever anyone around your business discusses anything that affects your consumers, they can use it to make better decisions in real time. This is the only path toward achieving true consumer centricity.

This book gives you the road map for doing that, but you'll need to make changes to the way you work. You'll transition from being a project manager to a strategic contributor. You'll understand why you need the right process and platform to ensure that data is accessible to those who need it, whenever they need it, and that it's well managed and integrated. You'll learn how to adapt yourself and others to this new market research landscape so that everyone feels positive about it. You'll discover what the future holds, so that you can prepare yourself for the profound shifts to come. If there's one thing we know, it's that, when the demands CEOs make of insights functions increase, professionals who are ahead of the game will be the ones to thrive.

We'd like to make a couple of points here. First, in this book, we use the terms "market research" and "consumer insights" interchangeably. They mean pretty much the same thing, but we use both to add variety. Second, while we tell the story of PepsiCo's transformation throughout to anchor our points, we also give you other examples. They're drawn from Zappi's client base because they're the businesses that we know the best, but they're not the only companies who are reshaping the way they do market research. We hope that you want to become one of them—you'll be in good company.

Despite the fact that we've hit you with a set of daunting problems, they actually amount to a huge opportunity—one that, if you take up the challenge, will make your role more fulfilling, your position more secure, and, just as importantly, enable your work to drive key decisions throughout your business. Marketers constantly develop new solutions and ideas. Consumer insights, if you do it right, can empower creators with data about what works and what doesn't, connecting your company with the culture it serves.

We hope that sounds exciting, but to be honest, this opportunity is going to land whether you like it or not. You can choose to maintain the status quo, convincing yourself that change won't impact you or that it's not relevant to your organization. Or you can position yourself in front of the change and be one of the people leading the way. Let's embark on this journey now.

> To access our FREE video series on Connected Insights, visit connectedinsights.com

PART ONE
THE CASE FOR CHANGE

ONE

Driving Competitive Advantage

What does consumer centricity mean for you? How do you translate that concept into the way you find and deliver consumer insights? Much of it comes down to working in an agile way. To understand why being agile is the key to unlocking consumer centricity, you must understand why market research needs to change.

There are two factors to consider. The first is that marketing has become a real-time game and, as a result, your current sequential ways of working are no longer adequate. Instead of taking a one-off brief, briefing an agency, and delivering results, you need to create ways of working with built-in learning loops that infuse consumer centricity into every commercial decision-making process.

The second factor to consider is that the main advantage large companies used to enjoy—that of scale—is now largely gone. Digitalization and other changes mean that assets like a huge distribution arm or a network of factories no longer provide protection against competitors. Big companies do have two remaining trump cards—a recognizable brand and large amounts of consumer research data—but even with these, there's a catch. The data is only useful if it can be leveraged, and at the moment it's sitting in silos where it's used only once. You need to build a market research machine that has consumer centricity at the core and allows you to discover what consumers at any time and place think about your categories—at low cost, super-fast. In other words, you can't afford to outsource your consumer intimacy muscle anymore.

We're getting ahead of ourselves, though. Before we explore how you can change the way you work, let's take a quick journey back in time to how things used to be. Over the last three decades, the insights industry has evolved from using phone surveys and mail-in questionnaires to using online panels, tools harnessing AI, and other technology in an effort to answer business questions from vast swaths of raw consumer data.

Back in the 1990s, one of our authors, Steve, found himself in conversation with a senior marketer from a large organization. The marketer told him that he viewed consumer insights as "the marketer's accountant." Steve didn't exactly embrace that label because he knew that market researchers were much more than number crunchers. They could inspire people to make better business decisions, not just validate ideas. He had to acknowledge, though, that there was a hint of truth in the description. The primary sources of marketing data during that time were surveys and focus groups; these were the only ways that marketers could get a glimpse into consumers' minds. Of course, there was also sales data, but that arrived beyond the stage at which ideas could be changed. More importantly, it didn't explain *why* people bought or didn't buy products, just how and where. Only consumer insights could shed light on the "why" and suggest tangible ways to improve things.

What's more, even though market research departments were central to any business decision that needed access to customer data, the process of acquiring that data was laborious and expensive. Talking to consumers meant either calling them by phone or hitting the streets. A project could take up to eight weeks to complete and cost around twenty times more than it does now, once interviewers were paid.

By the 2000s, this work shifted to online panels, which halved timescales and reduced costs, though it was still relatively slow and costly compared to today. This meant that opinions about consumer insights among marketers were divided. If obtaining data was such a hassle, some asked, why not rely on gut instinct instead? This, they felt, was more reliable. They weren't entirely wrong, because innovative concepts have always been a challenge to research. Back when the fax machine was only a glimmer in a product developer's eye, consumers said that they'd never use it because if a document needed to travel fast, they'd put it on a bike. Yet before long, fax machines were standard in every office around the world.

Other marketers took a different stance. They figured that if they were spending time and money on research, they'd better put it to good use. While this might seem like the more sensible choice, the insights often ended up being treated as a safety net: "Before I put this ad out, I'd better test it just to prove I've got consumer input. That way, if it fails, at least I can say I did the right thing." Insights were also used to settle internal disputes about what direction to take: "Let's consult the consumers—they can't be wrong." The adage that a marketer uses consumer insights data like a drunk uses a lamp post—for support rather than illumination—wasn't far from reality.

The shift to data abundance

Between 2000 and 2010, an array of other data streams, each offering an abundance of information, began to appear on the dashboards of consumer insights professionals and marketers. Social media was the main one. Imagine that you were in the ice cream business; you could now monitor how consumers were talking about your product online. What was their favorite "ice cream moment"? Who were they enjoying it with? What aspects did they love about it? What was more, not only could you discover how people were consuming your product, but you could also glean insights into their interests, lifestyles, and motivations. In other words, you could build a rich picture of *why* they were buying and eating your ice cream, not just read what they said in answer to your questions.

There was also clickstream data from a multitude of other online sources. What ice cream varieties were consumers clicking on while grocery shopping online? Did they visit your ice cream website? If so, how did they interact with it? What search terms did they use? Added to that came new forms of experience management data, which gradually overtook traditional customer satisfaction surveys. Brands started using technology to capture real-time feedback so that they could optimize their services as quickly as possible.

From these sources, marketers and consumer insights professionals constructed a three-dimensional impression of their customers, drawing on information from a variety of channels, such as websites, online ads, social media platforms, and retailers. It's no wonder that, at that time, there was talk of these data streams overtaking survey data or even eclipsing it altogether. In 2012, Steve attended a consumer insights conference that featured six speakers, none of whom were there to talk about surveys—only online data. That's how consumed marketing had become by this trend.

The thing about this new abundance of online data, though, was that marketers (and market researchers themselves) didn't necessarily see it as market research. Clickstream, social media, and ad data were often sold direct to marketing, while customer experience data was directed toward operations; none of it fell under the management of consumer insights departments. This gave marketers lots of ways to analyze their consumers, but the data they had access to was fragmented and unfiltered.

A good example of this lack of joined-up thinking in data collection was the contrast between the pre- and postlaunch processes of gathering consumer insights for a new product or campaign. The postlaunch data came in via digital channels such as sales figures, in-store customer satisfaction surveys, and social listening. The prelaunch data, however, entered the business in the form of disparate PowerPoint decks that sat on people's hard drives. There was, and still is, an imbalance between data that improves experiences and data that improves ideas.

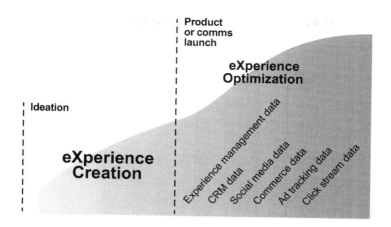

The split between available data streams before and after a product or comms launch. Brands are served with copious tools that help them understand how to optimize ads, but there is a massive imbalance between technology that optimizes in-market ads and data that improves ideas.

Despite the challenges caused by data coming from different sources and flowing into different parts of the business, it was undeniably beneficial that faster and more cost-effective ways of understanding consumer thinking were now available. This made it easier for marketers to use consumer insights more often; the trend for real-time, budget-friendly, and dynamic data generation persists to this day. Where some businesses might once have considered bypassing market research due to costs and timescales, the advent of online data sources made that approach increasingly unthinkable. Of course, market research should still be an input into business decisions and not a decider in and of itself—that hasn't changed. Once we were living in a world of abundant insights, however, decision makers could work in a more well-informed way and enjoy direct access to data like never before.

Where being agile comes in

Although the transition from manual to digital made the data generation process faster and more cost effective, it didn't change the fundamentals of handling data when it reaches the market research department—and it still hasn't. There's been no broad-scale reimagining of the way that market researchers leverage data or who has access to it in the way that PepsiCo has done. It's still a project-based process that is controlled by and limited to the consumer insights function and puts the brakes on potential responsiveness to marketers' needs. While consumer centricity demands that marketers have the consumer "in the room" at all times, market research data is consistently late to the meeting.

This puts you, in the insights function, in a difficult position. If social media and other online data are scattered around the business, and project-managed market research surveys—one of the most reliable methods of predicting consumer preferences—are slow and cumbersome, how can your company become more consumer centric? For that, the right people (wherever they are in your organization) must have access to holistic data whenever they need it. The word we're using to describe this concept is "agile."

"Agile" is one of those words that can mean different things to different people. It initially stemmed from IT, so let's look at how we interpret it. Do you remember the way that IT projects used to be run, before agile was a thing? IT project managers spent weeks engaging with stakeholders to understand what they wanted from a new system. They'd create a detailed specification, and a year down the line they'd return to those stakeholders and show them what they'd built. By that time, the world had moved on and the original project was only partially relevant—if at all. Tough luck for the stakeholders and for the business.

That was the old approach. Today, IT projects follow agile principles, where project managers engage with stakeholders every few weeks throughout the development process:

> "I've implemented that feature you requested. Does it help? Great. Should I focus on the tasks we initially planned for the next two weeks?"
>
> "No, your priorities have changed."
>
> "OK, what's important to you now?"

As the above exchange implies, if project managers consult everyone regularly rather than presenting the result as a done deal, the new system will be more valuable.

Marketing has gone through its own agile transformation, too. Back in the 1990s, a brand manager in a consumer packaged goods company might launch a new product variant every couple of years and a new advertising campaign once a year. Although waiting several weeks for consumer feedback on their ad concepts was a pain, it wasn't the end of the world, since they had several months to create the ad. In today's landscape, a marketer might create fifty or sixty variations of an ad tailored to different audiences across various digital platforms, geographies, and interests. Moreover, to maximize relevance, those ads are tied to trends, events, or moments in the buyer journey.

Product development has been on a similar journey. Steve remembers managing market research projects in the past that determined whether a company invested $2 million on reconfiguring its factory for a new product line. Today, factories are more flexible, and brands are making products specifically for different retailers. Marketers are also bypassing product testing entirely, creating products and just seeing how they sell instead.

These staggering changes in marketing and manufacturing technology give marketers incredible opportunities to test and innovate. If marketers launch a social media ad, they receive A/B testing feedback within minutes. If they introduce a new product, they discover whether people are buying it the day it hits the stores. If they change the point of sale, their sales data tells them almost instantly whether it's increased sales.

But wait...

This is all great, but it doesn't take into account the following drawbacks:

- **Delayed feedback:** The sales and clickstream data that tell marketers about a product or ad's success arrive after the event. Until then, marketers are working "blind," leading to a wastage of time and resources on concepts that consumer insights might have told them were destined to fail. What's more, without data to inspire which new ads and products get created in the first place, concepts will always be confined to the imaginations of marketers and product developers. They'll also be subject to marketer biases because your average marketer is not your average consumer. Research data deepens companies' understanding of their consumers, and it should form the basis of creative ideas.

- **Lack of context:** Sales and clickstream data don't tell marketers *why* something has succeeded or failed. Consequently, marketers have little guidance for making informed decisions next time.

- **Brand risks:** When market research isn't used to shape ad development, a creative treatment can be released that's damaging for the brand.

It's clear that attitudinal data, which contains none of the above issues, still needs to be integrated into online data. The problem is that it hasn't kept pace with the instant access afforded by social media and clickstream data. Marketers need a holistic view of all their data in real time, not in a month. This problem is within your power to solve, but it requires you to do three things:

1. Rethink your processes to align them with the needs of decision makers around the organization, thereby ensuring that the data you collect serves their requirements in an agile way.

2. Move to a digitalized and democratized method of managing your data so that it's instantly accessible to anyone who needs it.

3. Become a strategic thinker rather than a project manager so that you have more value during the move to consumer centricity.

There's more. While being agile is necessary right now, there are two additional waves that will be crashing on your shore in the next couple of years. We hinted at one of these waves—data integration—when we discussed social media and clickstream data. At the moment, too few market researchers are integrating survey data with sales, social media, clickstream, and other online data. We're not just talking about making the data more convenient to look at by bringing it together in one place but about using your curious and analytical mind to create meaning from it in a way that only you can do.

The other wave is AI, which is already changing everything. In practical terms, AI will disrupt every phase of the research process. While people like you will still be essential for managing those processes, AI will take over a considerable proportion of the work that you currently do. Although this might sound scary, it also presents remarkable opportunities if you're willing to learn how to use it in the right way. In Chapter 6, we explore the implications of AI in more detail.

Do you know what you know?

AI is about to disrupt everything, but that's not all you need to think about. You're also missing out on the incredible power of meta-insights. There's an expression you may often hear in market research: "If only we knew what we know." In an age when every organization is adopting abundant data platforms and agile ways of working, data alone isn't a differentiator. It's how you use it that sets you apart. Ask yourself how much access you (or anyone else in your business) have to what you *already know*. What about the research projects that you've conducted over the past year or two, along with online data that's been streaming into your company? Where is that wealth of information now? Are you actively learning from it today, or is it going to waste? If you're reinventing the wheel every time you want to discover something new, you're not being agile.

PepsiCo has all its market research data in one place and a dedicated meta-analytics team that delivers insights from research already carried out. On top of this, their platform has a built-in learning loop, which means that every time someone in the business generates market research data, it's added to the platform and the whole business becomes smarter. This has revolutionized how efficiently and effectively their market research function delivers insights to the business.

McDonald's serves as another example of a company that has completely revised its approach to this aspect of market research. Like many mature businesses, McDonald's marketing challenge is how to retain a loyal customer base while simultaneously driving incremental visits and sales. If a customer visits a restaurant for lunch, can they be enticed to buy a coffee as well? Can they then be encouraged to return for dinner? To achieve this, McDonald's continually creates new products and menus, generating fresh opportunities for customers to make purchases.

In the past, McDonald's regularly carried out a lot of market research, but it was via large, legacy survey providers (who, as you know, are slow) and only at tent pole stages in time. What's more, they weren't leveraging what they already knew, so they were essentially learning the same lessons over and over again. They went from project to project or innovation to innovation without the technology or infrastructure to house, mine, and use what they'd discovered already. This led them to be an inefficient, and sometimes slow, innovator.

The consumer insights lead at McDonald's, Matt Cahill, recognized that they needed to carry out rapid prototyping in a more agile way, but it was complicated. The company operated in well over 100 countries across the world, but only a few of those had dedicated insights teams. They were accustomed to doing things a certain way, which meant that there was a degree of inertia when they were asked to change. As Matt and his team started to pilot more agile methods of obtaining insights in the United States, McDonald's biggest market, their new approach gained credibility. You'll learn in the next chapter how this played out, but for now it's worth knowing that it contributed to McDonald's outperforming the rest of its category—an amazing achievement.

You should be starting to recognize that gaining and providing easy access to the data you already have across the business are essential for becoming agile and consumer centric. In the next chapter, we'll delve more deeply into what this looks like in real life.

The takeaways

- Consumer research data has become faster, cheaper, and more abundant than it was twenty to thirty years ago.

- However, this speed and abundance haven't had an impact on how quickly holistic consumer insights are generated.

- Market research hasn't kept up with agile working practices in marketing or with the need for more consumer centricity.

- The consumer insights function needs to rethink its processes, become digitalized and democratized, and be more strategic.

- Past survey data isn't being mined to create meta-insights, meaning that consumer insights professionals have to continually reinvent the wheel.

- All these issues create slow data that's limited and incomplete.

Action points

- **Kick off a digitalization taskforce:** Amass a group of key, future-thinking colleagues who'll help you on your journey.

- **Pulse-check your data:** How much of it do you own? How well is it connected? What percentage of decisions happen with and without consumer data?

- **Assess the agility of your insights:** A good benchmark is that at least 50% of your projects take less than one week to complete.

- **Build bridges across your organization:** Find out who needs data but lacks access, who you can't reach in time and why, and who's using the wrong data.

- **Take all the consumer insights work done in the past year on a certain brand or category, and mine it for meta-learning:** Discover what it takes to develop those meta-insights and build a capability (a team and set of skills) around it to create ongoing competitive advantage.

> To request complimentary copies of this book for your team, visit connectedinsights.com

TWO

What Agile Market Research Looks Like

P epsiCo's journey toward becoming more agile in market research offers some valuable lessons. Stephan realized early on that his consumer insights function had always worked in an "identify the research need, brief the research team, then wait for the results" kind of way. He also knew that this was no longer acceptable in a world where marketing had become a real-time game. He saw that his teams needed tools that supported real-time decision making and enabled world-class marketing. Rather than waste time on endless vision and mission sessions, he decided to just start the change and, as he put it at the time, "act ourselves into new thinking."

Stephan started small by working to solve a frustration that all his market research leaders had with their early innovation testing methodology. As we mentioned, the solution to this was Zappi's digital platform, a tool that enabled marketers to access modeled data and insights on demand at local and global scales. Crucially, it did this in a super-fast way while making the data scattered around PepsiCo's various islands available centrally. This reduced duplication, and therefore time and cost, and freed up many hours for Stephan's insights teams, who didn't need to commission new research when existing data could already give them the answers. The platform provided meta-analysis so that insights people could learn what they already knew, as well as testing new assumptions and hypotheses using primary research. Moreover, because insights teams and others around the business could use the data whenever they wanted, PepsiCo, rather than their external vendors, had full ownership of it.

Over time, PepsiCo's consumer insights professionals grew confident that the new platform gave them a powerful conduit for joined-up information and that it made a tangible impact on the business. Although they still lived on their separate islands, they now did a lot of their work using the same platform. This marked a profound shift from working alone to working collectively in a way that made everyone feel more connected. Just as importantly, marketers around PepsiCo were starting to see the benefits of this joined-up way of operating. A Doritos marketer in Brazil, for instance, had direct access to the platform and could learn from consumer feedback across multiple Doritos ads worldwide. The more ads the platform tested, the smarter and more granular the resulting insights became.

It's worth spending a moment to appreciate what this transformation gave to PepsiCo. There's an old saying that you can ask for something that's good, quick, or cheap, but you'll never get all three—two if you're lucky. By surfing the wave of digitalization, however, the company's insights team could have them all. Marketers and consumer insights teams could dramatically improve the quality of their work because the data was harmonized, standardized, and globalized. This allowed them to share their insights and create meta-learnings that benefited everyone. They could carry out research projects in a day instead of three weeks, and they could do it for a third of what they'd spent with their previous vendors because they'd leveraged their scale and simplified their processes.

Today, PepsiCo's platform has expanded to the point that it's removed the "go-between" of vendor management from the equation in day-to-day research tasks. While Stephan and Kate's teams do consult with traditional research agencies for ad hoc projects, they are not reliant on them for fast-moving creative projects. In addition to innovation and ad testing powered by Zappi, PepsiCo incorporates tools from other companies for functions such as social listening, trend prediction, demand space, market segmentation, trend research, and claims testing. Just as importantly, it's instilled a sense of self-belief in the company's market research people. They feel more empowered than before, enabling them to be braver when needed. No longer seeing themselves as project managers for research tasks, they're willing to challenge and question the briefs they receive. They're more intentional, which means that instead of viewing a project in isolation, they have in mind its end business objective. They have the confidence to keep things simple. Because they're working with a standardized platform, they don't have to reinvent the wheel each time there's a need for data, and it's easier for them to avoid information overload.

After a while, Stephan's background in marketing and brand management led him to recognize that he needed to name the platform. Senior Director of Global Insights (and one of our authors) Kate Schardt came up with an idea when she was reading her daughters a bedtime story about famous women inventors: "Ada," after Ada Lovelace, a pioneering nineteenth-century mathematician and the world's first computer programmer. Today, the name isn't just a label, it's a unifying reference for people around PepsiCo whenever they talk about the platform. For instance, at their global category meetings, marketers say things like "These are the Ada scores," or "From Ada, we learned this." Ada has become a single source of truth they can turn to for advice and information.

The adoption of Ada has grown the insights function's reputation within PepsiCo. To gauge its impact,

Stephan's team carries out an annual global survey asking marketers and business leaders whether consumer insights are giving more value. Survey responses have shown a significant improvement in the last three years: The proportion of respondents who consider their consumer insights colleagues to be indispensable business partners has risen from 74% to 85%; the proportion who think that their insights business partners put the consumer at the heart of all decision making has gone from 73% to 82%; and the proportion who believe that their insights partners demonstrate a deep understanding of their business challenges has risen from 78% to 85%. These results reflect an acknowledgment of the role that insights now play in driving consumer-focused strategies.

What have you taken from PepsiCo's journey? Has it helped you to visualize what a connected way of working looks like? If you do things right, you can transform how market research is used in your organization and influence every consumer-related decision it makes.

You can see from PepsiCo's story that a connected approach to market research has some important features:

- **Real-time operation:** It works alongside agile decision making in the rest of the business.

- **Digital platform foundation:** It's based on a platform that both generates its own survey data and integrates relevant data from other areas of the business. That way, it transforms scattered data into a harmonized, standardized, and globally accessible resource using the right metrics, benchmarks, and contexts.

- **Accessibility:** It liberates consumer data from silos and makes it available to any relevant person in the organization, whenever they need it. This democratization ensures that insights can influence decisions at every level and encourages a unified approach to understanding consumers.

- **Self-improving:** It talks to itself, thereby creating a learning loop that contributes to the organization's collective intelligence over time. In other words, every time we test an ad somewhere, all of us get smarter.

Agile, digital, democratic, and self-improving: This is how things should be from now on. We've covered the concept of agile, so let's explore being digital and democratic next.

The new digital democracy

In most businesses, the data that informs the work of marketers and product developers comes either direct to marketers (in the case of online data streams) or via the gatekeeper of the consumer insights department (in the case of primary research).

This, as PepsiCo's experience shows, is an outdated process. It's too slow for today's agile world and doesn't harness the wealth of data buried in slide decks on people's hard drives. Moreover, it involves a trade-off between speed and accuracy: Online data provides immediacy but lacks some of the objectivity required for fully informed decision making, while survey data is valuable but incomplete without real-time, online insights. What PepsiCo has done instead is to remove the silos between these data sources and use them as complementary data streams that together create an actionable, real-time view of consumers.

Digital integration

To transcend these limitations, there's a need to consolidate and analyze all the data sources so that they become more than the sum of their individual parts. Usually, the only business function doing this is the IT department. While IT people are skilled at aligning data assets, they don't have the market research expertise needed to extract meaningful insights from them. Only insights people can bring context to the data and connect it so that it catches the business in stride. This isn't a new frustration; we imagine that both you and your marketing colleagues have long tried to find ways around this problem.

The solution lies in adopting an integrated digital platform. It should be one that allows you to interrogate and learn from all the consumer data coming into your business from any source and grants you access to data that you already have so you don't have to repeat what's already been done. It should be one that enables you to answer pressing business questions without delay and see the gaps in your knowledge so that you can decide what new surveys you need to fill them. Finally, it should be one that uses the resulting data to become smarter still. This might seem like an unachievable goal, but in the second part of this book we'll walk you through how to go about it.

As we touched on in Chapter 1, McDonald's went on this journey when their market research team implemented a digital solution that helped them assess whether a product innovation was going to drive incremental sales. With their new platform, they could input menu variants at different price points, swiftly receive feedback, and, just as importantly, retain what they learned for future use. At first, some people around the business were skeptical about whether it would work, so the team kept the old methods running alongside the new tool to see if the new one generated the same results. Over time it became clear that it did, and because the new platform was so much more agile and useful, the original faded away.

Once the new platform was accepted, McDonald's underwent a shift toward iterative learning and became quicker at pushing innovations into the market. With their newfound ability to retain data in the platform as they went along, the market research team was able to move from revalidating previously tested concepts to leveraging data instantly and using it to come up with ideas. This saved them both time and money.

One of the best examples of how this platform gave McDonald's much faster access to early-stage insights was its use in what they called the "chicken sandwich wars." The chicken sandwich had long been viewed as a specialty product offered by only a handful of brands when a viral moment related to Popeyes' newly introduced chicken sandwich drew Chick-fil-A's ire on social media. A subsequent short-lived craze resulted in Popeyes seeing a 38% increase in sales at the end of the year. Suddenly, every brand sought to carve out their own niche in the market.[2]

Seeking to introduce a new chicken sandwich to their menu, McDonald's created a concept board featuring various brand offerings for consumer testing. Because there were several other brands with more long-term credibility in the chicken sandwich space, McDonald's scored a disappointing seventh out of eight brands. As soon as they learned that, they opted to bypass further concept testing and concentrate their efforts purely on product development. They knew that their product had to be not only good, but inherently different if it

---

2   P Cobe, "A brief history of the chicken sandwich wars", Restaurant Business Online (January 7, 2021), www.restaurantbusinessonline.com/food/brief-history-chicken-sandwich-wars, accessed March 27, 2024

was to win over consumers, and after expending a huge amount of energy on it they came up with a version that excelled. This is a great illustration of how quick access to research results helps a business to strip away distractions and focus its efforts on what will bring it success. Early learning, together with a bold strategic approach, gave McDonald's a clear road map to bring the McCrispy™ to market.

The democratic shift

Building an agile platform is easy, but getting people to use it is what determines its success. One way of encouraging widespread usage is to democratize access to it. This can mean different things for different organizations, and how far you take it depends on your culture, team structure, markets, and reach. What's most important is that your research tool meets people on their own terms.

For PepsiCo, democratization is based on two things. One is that removing the go-between has empowered the company's consumer insights users, and the other is that the platform uses standardized processes and measurements. Insights teams, with marketing leaders, still lead the consumer research process, but they can put much faster results into the hands of marketing because suppliers no longer drive the engagement. They're also upskilling themselves to be fully responsible for the outcome of their research. They no longer hide behind vendors when it comes to ad or innovation testing, their methodology is standardized, and the data speaks for itself. That means insights managers need to engage with findings and the resulting recommendations themselves as an integral part of the process of building effective advertising. For many, this change has been a welcome opportunity for insights leaders to increase their impact and influence, leading to greater overall job satisfaction and empowerment.

Global wine and spirits producer Pernod Ricard is another example of a business that's adopted a more democratic approach to data access.[3] It is a decentralized holding company made up of a global flagship in France, autonomous affiliates, and brands around the world. Originally, they had a market research function that worked with large external providers, and everything was slow. To enhance the strategic role of their consumer insights function, they knew that they had to find a way to give their hundreds of brand managers access to consumer insights tools on their desks. This would mean that, when the brand managers were planning promotional campaigns or new products, they'd have a way to quickly validate their instincts rather than waiting for the head office in Paris to come back to them.

Pernod Ricard's solution was to implement a digital platform that enabled the business to test ads and

---

3   R Barry, "Democratizing insights in a decentralized organization", Zappi (2022), www.zappi.io/web/podcast/democratizing-insights-in-a-decentralized-organization, accessed March 27, 2024

promotions on the fly. While brand managers retained the strategic input of the market research team, they also had direct access to data.[4] But this didn't mean insights professionals handed over the keys to the platform. Incorporating their own "freedom within a framework" mindset, the Pernod Ricard insights team created clearly defined guardrails so marketers could pick preselected audiences and create surveys. This enabled them to work quickly to get the consumer data they needed.

When the change was implemented, the consumer insights team collaborated with its platform provider, Zappi, to train marketers all over the world to use it in a way that preserved the consumer insights' objectivity. In other words, marketers weren't able to "grade their own homework," but they were able to come in on a Tuesday morning and use the market research data to make decisions about how to position their campaigns. This approach proved highly successful and has now been adopted globally, expanding to include packaging, new concept ideas, and promotions. As a result, the insights team has become a lot more strategically focused because less of their time is sucked into managing tactical projects.

Democratization isn't about gatekeeping data but giving people the tools to make human-centric decisions with insights. This shift requires a significant change

---

4   Zappi, "Pernod Ricard proves it's possible to democratize insights", Zappi (2022), www.zappi.io/web/customer-stories/pernod-ricard-proves-its-possible-to-democratize-insights, accessed March 27, 2024

of mindset. With data as the "new oil," whoever has information has power, right? While your aim has always been to ensure that data is wisely used, it's power nonetheless.

Here's the thing, though. When you work with a platform that's accessible to anyone who needs it, you still have power—just of a different (and superior) kind. Marketers will always want your help with difficult and strategic questions, and you are uniquely positioned to connect cultural, trend, survey, and qualitative viewpoints. It's your job to use data to tell the stories of what consumers want both now and in the future, and your ability to infuse human sentiment into the numbers will drive innovation throughout the business. Through this combination of data democratization and your strategic input, consumer insights will become a critical source of competitive advantage for your company.

SoFi is one of the fastest-growing financial institutions in the United States, built on the idea of helping consumers get their money right. They understand the value of customer centricity and have democratized consumer insights to the point where there's no central insights team dictating the flow of information. Instead, SoFi puts consumer research directly into the hands of brand managers, so insights are accessible when needed.[5]

---

5   R Barry, "Landing insights without an insights team", Zappi (2022), www.zappi.io/web/podcast/landing-insights-without-an-insights-team, accessed May 29, 2024

Are you starting to see how digitalization and democratization of data go hand in hand? Agile working is driving the need for a move away from a command and control approach toward a democratic one. To provide democratic access, a digital platform that all relevant people can use is essential, as it's the only way that you can put information in front of them in real time. Such a platform can also integrate all your data sources, including preexisting data, so that the insights everyone gains are more predictive than before. There is no one-size-fits-all approach to democratization, but by understanding when, how, and where insights are utilized by teams in a connected way, you can build a framework that works for you.

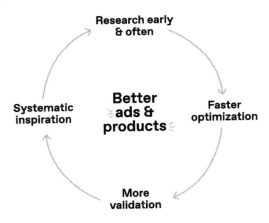

How a digital, democratic market research platform helps you become agile

Why this change is worth your while

This transition may seem daunting, so it's worth highlighting the enormous benefits of this new way of working.

- **Process efficiency:** Standardization of research templates makes it easier to compare data from different projects, resulting in more useful insights. It also focuses resources on value-added work, versus checking yet another questionnaire. These efficiencies have a snowball effect. By bringing in more research early in the creative process, you can optimize more quickly, do more validation, and inspire new ideas at speed without turning to traditional research suppliers.

- **Innovation enablement:** You stop putting the brakes on innovation when you don't have to duplicate research that's been done before. Instead, you can tap into existing data through your platform, saving both time and resources. While PepsiCo's knowledge management platform, Ask-Ada, provides access to research that was done before, that doesn't mean that it is consistently used to the fullest by marketing and insights leaders. New technology such as AI will make data even more accessible in the future.

- **Connected insights:** Marketers gain access to agile insights whenever they need them. This leads to more effective products and campaigns, which drive better business outcomes.

- **Strategic involvement:** With less time spent on project management tasks, you have space to involve yourself in strategic business decisions. This elevation of your role positions market research as a central driver of consumer-focused strategies and your expertise as a key source of your company's competitive advantage.

The three stages of consumer insights maturity—from order taker to business partner

That's what an agile market research department looks like, but how many actually meet those standards? There's a wide variation in how far different consumer insights functions have traveled on the path to agility and consumer centricity. What about yours? Is it partway along, in touching distance of the end destination, or right at the start with no sign of movement at all? Change never happens overnight, so it can be helpful to see the process as a series of stages.

To outline the evolving role of market research departments in large organizations, Zappi introduced the

Connected Insights framework.[6] Having worked with thousands of brands over the years to centralize their insights and increase insights maturity, Zappi has observed the path market research must take to be essential to the business and integral to its competitive advantage.

There are three stages of consumer insights maturity, reflecting both the ways that data and technology are utilized by a business and the impact and perception of insights teams. In Zappi's experience, most teams fall into either Stages One or Two. Insights teams who have reached Stage Three are rare, but those that have are able to work faster and substantially improve the effectiveness of their advertising and product development. As you read through the stages, think about which level best reflects the role of market research in your organization right now.

Stage One: Disconnected

According to Zappi's research and experience, this is the level at which the majority of insights departments are stuck. At this stage, teams are seen as order takers; their work is project-based and led by the demands of budget holders in other departments. As a result, their influence and impact are limited. Most senior

---

6   Zappi, "The Connected Insights framework", Zappi (2022), www.zappi.io/web/a/connected-insights-framework, accessed May 30, 2024

executives around the company don't give these kinds of consumer insights departments much thought.

Stage Two: Fragmented

Many insights teams operate at Stage Two. In this phase, they are beginning to connect one project, or perhaps one team or brand, to another, but have not yet systematically connected all of these disparate pieces. For this reason, they cannot influence strategy or rise to executive-level visibility. In other words, at this stage, insights professionals are seen as advisers; it's at the discretion of budget holders to decide whether to involve insights professionals.

At this stage, however, teams are also becoming more strategic and valuable to the company. They have more support from senior marketers, but they still don't set their own priorities or have their own budgets.

Stage Three: Connected

Only a small fraction of market research departments are operating at this level. They've gained the trust of senior executives to the degree that those executives believe the consumer insights team is strategic, demonstrates critical thinking, and serves as a trusted adviser toward the organization's higher-level business goals. This partnership approach is starting to create a culture of learning that's increasingly adept at anticipating, not just retrospectively evaluating, customers' needs. One of the key features of Stage Three is that research results are shared throughout the organization and not just kept in the research department; this promotes collaboration.

At Stage Three, consumer insights departments are connected across projects, brands, and geographies. They are tied together seamlessly, without any gaps between phases of the creative and development processes. As a result, they can drive best-in-class innovation and foresight and make more intelligent predictions using centralized and connected data repositories. As a result, they are trusted to manage larger budgets company-wide. At this stage, the function excels at giving perspective on important trends, and its leaders often have executive roles reporting directly to a C-level executive, such as a Chief Marketing Officer (CMO). The insights team is an integral part of the business decision-making process and is seen as a world-class thought leader rather than a project manager.

Market researchers on Stage Three teams are the equivalent of business partners, with PepsiCo's consumer insights function as a prime example. When consumer insights are fully connected, they are integral to the company's decision making and contribute to its competitive edge. As you assess your own insights department's level of maturity, you can see the journey you'll need to go on if you're to become a business partner yourself.

	LEVEL 1
STATE OF INSIGHTS	DISCONNECTED
ORGANIZATIONAL MATURITY	ORDER TAKERS
PEOPLE	› Individual contributors › Project managers › Reactive insights
PROCESS	› Insights commissioned on a project basis › High dependency on outsourcing for validation › Agencies used for project management
PLATFORM	› Technology either not used or used for singular projects › Tech partners are disconnected from business goals › Disparate and decentralized
DATA	› Consumers are consulted occasionally › Data is disconnected › Insights are single use
CONSUMER FOCUS	› Organizational use of insights is limited › Point-in-time business impact › On the periphery of decision making

The Connected Insights Framework

LEVEL 2

FRAGMENTED

ADVISERS

- › Proactively engage with stakeholders
- › Teams contribute to insights
- › Overseen by insights leader, separate from marketing

- › Inconsistent – project-based and programmatic in separate work streams
- › Medium dependency on outsourcing
- › Agencies used for program management

- › Used for multiple projects
- › Separate, siloed platforms for different purposes
- › Platforms are shared by more than one team

- › Data is siloed
- › Access to insights starts to become shared
- › Repeatable but disconnected cadence

- › Consumers are consulted frequently
- › Business decisions informed by data
- › Consumers are reflected in decision making

LEVEL 3

CONNECTED

STRATEGIC PARTNERS

- › Insights teams partner with stakeholders
- › Highly collaborative and visible
- › Proactively upskilled

- › Systematic processes
- › Connected data to optimize ideas
- › Agencies generate connected data, guided by insights business partner

---

- › Used across all projects at each stage
- › Centralized system for all data
- › Core part of team management process

- › Connected across projects, brands, and teams
- › Democratized to the whole organization
- › Meta-learnings to leverage historic data

- › Consumers are consulted in every stage of projects
- › Continuous impact for sustained competitive advantage
- › Consumers at the heart of decision making

To download a full-color PDF, visit connectedinsights.com

How you should work toward Stage Three

If you want market research to be indispensable to your organization's success, Stage Three is what you should aim for. When you get there, you'll spend your time focusing on understanding consumers, just like you always have. The difference will be that you'll take your knowledge to the rest of the business to help it grow. Reaching that point means letting go of being a project manager and embracing the use of technology to digitalize, automate, and curate data. It shouldn't be your job to manage projects and spend hours translating data into slide decks, but it should be your job to analyze how that data influences the product and brand road map in the following quarters or years. You can only do this if your workload is dominated not by projects but by innovation and getting smarter at delivering insights to those who need it, when they need it. Market research professionals who set themselves up for Stage Three have three qualities:

- They think programs, not projects.
- They update their methodologies.
- They leverage existing learnings.

Think programs, not projects

Your job is to serve consumers by using data to solve business problems, not write briefs. You do that by building an insights ecosystem that integrates data with the people who need to use it. This means:

- **Digitalizing everything:** This includes not only your surveys and research tools, but also your workflows. If you automate whatever you can, you'll reduce the burden of project management.

- **Standardizing your audiences, markets, success metrics, tools, and taxonomies:** This ensures that all your data is comparable. It also avoids the problem of using a different sample frame every time you run a new project, and repeating the same questions (to which you already have the answers).

- **Finding a few partners and getting close to them:** You need suppliers who'll work with each other so that they can help you build an integrated picture of your consumers.

- **Knowing how your company measures success:** This can be a challenge in that you might not have access to the information, but if you can include success metrics in the standardized insights framework that you're building, you can be of more value to your company.

- **Dropping the gatekeeper role:** You need to build closer relationships with the departments you serve, but to do that you have to let them use some of your tools. This requires a leap of faith, but it takes many projects off your to-do list.

Update methodologies

You can't just digitalize old-world methodologies, because those methodologies were created for a context that doesn't exist anymore. Consumer insights professionals who go on this journey find that the following are fundamental to their success:

- **Thin-slicing the research:** Because of the time and cost involved in doing surveys, it's tempting to cram in as many questions as you can, but in the agile world it makes more sense to focus on one business question. Rather than including a concept test, a packaging test, and discrete choice models in the same survey, you can parse these perspectives out over multiple touch points. This also helps to improve data quality, so you get highly engaged responses over ten questions instead of distracted responses over thirty.

- **Using mobile:** More and more online surveys are done on mobile, so your platform needs to fit the medium. That means no more grids and thirty-minute surveys, or you'll only be talking to the kind of consumers who have the time and motivation to work through long questionnaires on their computers.

- **Keeping calibrating:** Run calibration exercises with trusted vendors where you use existing insights to calibrate against what you know works in the market. This is a great tool for setting yourself free from project management. You can build your own prediction models based on your unique success metrics.

Leverage existing learnings

You want to get to a point where you can be more predictive about your consumers, campaigns, and brands. This involves:

- **Having a connected repository of information:** This ensures that you don't have to keep managing projects that give you answers you already have (somewhere). It allows you to build foresight because you're not spending time and money reinventing the wheel. The first thing you'll do when someone gives you a brief is show them how to check it against existing research.

- **Creating guardrails:** Start from what you already know works, so that your internal customers can avoid wasting time making the same mistakes over and over.

- **Encouraging a change in attitude from other departments:** You know how it goes. Marketing doesn't get the stimulus together in time for testing, and agencies throw creative at you too late to test. The problem doesn't all come from your end. You can be part of the best market research team in the world, but if the business doesn't change its behavior collectively, you won't make the progress that's needed. The consumer insights professional who encourages culture change partners up with vendors, ad agency teams, and creative partners to bring them into the fold.

We hope that you feel enthusiastic about this brave new world, but we expect you have a lot of questions about how you're going to make it happen. That's what we'll explore in Part Two.

The takeaways

- Creating a digital platform to analyze your data means that you can access data from any source, including data you already have, in one place.

- When new data is added to the platform, it creates a learning loop that makes the whole business smarter over time.

- Culture determines democratization. Your vision for agile insights should work within your company culture and structure, not seek to reinvent it.

- When you stop being a project manager, you can start being a strategist and make market research a key part of your organization's competitive advantage.

- The consumer insights professional of the future updates their methodologies, focuses on the long term, and thinks about programs, not projects.

Action points

- **Look at how consumer insights currently fit into your creative process:** What standards are in place, and how are research projects catalyzed?

- **Document potential benefits:** What could a market research process and platform like PepsiCo's give your consumer insights function in terms of influence within your business?

- **Consider a recent large marketing campaign:** How could you have made it better if you'd had a more agile and integrated platform to work with?

- **Consider the stakeholders:** Ask yourself how such a platform might be received by different stakeholders around your organization.

- **Track how you spend your time:** Create an idealistic view of how you should be spending it and compare that to what actually happens.

- **Audit your access points:** Look critically at how you're approached—or passed over—by marketing and product departments. Where do they most often engage you and where do they look the other way?

PART TWO
BUILDING AN AGILE MARKET RESEARCH FUNCTION

THREE

Your Process

Earlier we discussed the fact that, in a data-driven world, you find yourself inundated with information pouring in from a multitude of sources, akin to a bunch of fire hoses turned up to full blast. You understand the importance of using this wealth of data to drive business decisions, whether naming a new product or the price point at which it's sold. You also know that data must reach the right people at the right time, and that, depending on your company culture and setup, decision makers should have the autonomy to generate their own research so that they have timely insights precisely when they need them.

How can you attain this ideal scenario? How do you corral all those data streams and harness their potential for you and anyone else who could benefit from them? In addition, how do you ensure that past market research data is as accessible as the most recent project you commissioned? The answer is that you need a platform: an architectural framework powered by technology that consolidates and organizes data, enabling people to analyze and learn from it in an agile way. This platform must be as simple, flexible, and efficient as possible.

To develop such a *platform*, however, you need first to map out a meticulous *process* that will define a set of design criteria for it. Designing one that will cater to everyone's needs means understanding where the data comes from, who should take responsibility for it, who should have access to it (along with how and when), why they require it, and how they intend to use it. While you're doing that, you also have to take into account the *people* who'll be using it, whether they are you and your team in market research or others around the business. These three elements—process, platform, and people—are interdependent and, to a certain extent, overlapping, so in some ways it's artificial to split them apart. Yet it's also important to give each their due, which is why this chapter focuses on your process, the next one on your platform, and the one after that on people.

The golden triangle of digital insights transformation

Let's see how process, platform, and people work in unison. Think of them as a golden triangle representing the three domains that you need to change if you're to create a new, agile way of doing market research. The *process* informs the platform's design, the *platform* (or tools and technology) makes the process work in real life, and the *people* use the process and platform to generate business results. Over time, feedback from users may lead to adjustments to both the process and the platform.

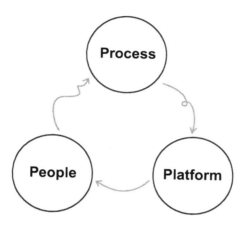

The golden triangle of process, platform, and people

Process

A process is a set of repeatable steps leading to a desired goal. To create your integrated market research process, you must first define the goals you want to support. For example, brand managers might want to know how well their ad concepts are performing or to view their sales volumes for product variants in different regions. Once you know your goals, you can determine responsibilities, timelines, and what journeys the data needs to go on to meet those objectives. We will explore your process in this chapter.

Platform

A platform is the combination of technologies and tools that bring a process to life. Many businesses make the mistake of implementing flashy technology without having a sound process in place, but the best approach is first to understand the problem you aim to solve and the goals you want to achieve, and then to design a platform that aligns with them. We delve into platforms in Chapter 4.

People

It's people who will execute the tasks within your process and use your platform. They could be market research personnel responsible for creating the templates and frameworks to generate survey data and other reports, or they could be users around the business, such as marketers and sales teams. Regardless of their role, if they don't know how to use the platform, they won't gain the right data from it to inform their decisions. This will mean training and supporting them until they feel confident enough to get the best out of it. It will also require your winning their buy-in at the outset; otherwise, you'll see slow adoption and suboptimal usage. We explore the role of people in Chapter 5.

For a consumer insights infrastructure to function effectively, all three elements must work harmoniously, just like a stable, three-legged stool. If any leg is shorter than the others, the stool will fall over. Without a tightly defined process, the platform that's based on it won't be aligned correctly and people won't work efficiently. This could lead them to lose faith in the platform and revert to their old ways. Conversely, a great process without an equally great platform won't translate into real-life effectiveness. If people don't know how to use the platform properly, or feel negatively toward it, your company won't gain a return on its investment in the technology, and everyone will lose out. The key to success is finding the right balance between these three critical areas.

PepsiCo's approach

From the outset, Stephan and Kate wanted to build an entirely new market research toolkit. They also knew that, in the hypercompetitive world of consumer packaged goods, they first needed to focus on the areas where consumer input was most vital and the largest volume of research was already being carried out. These were advertising development and product innovation. With advertising development, they wanted to replace the existing methodology for researching TV ads while also extending it to cover digital ads, where the spend increasingly went.

With these priorities in mind, they carefully identified the key moments in the advertising process where consumer data would provide the greatest value in optimizing the company's campaigns. They initially concentrated on later-stage testing, such as finished films, and mid-stage testing, such as animatics, to build a predictive model against media ROI. They have since added an earlier-stage tool called Storyboard. With their legacy systems, it was slow and expensive to test animatics. The new platform they envisaged, however, would allow them to seek consumer input in a more sustainable way at every critical stage in the advertising development process. This was especially important before the campaign went too far for marketers to make meaningful changes. This shift in approach highlighted the need for a suite of tools that could provide data using research stimuli that were relevant to any part of the process, such as questionnaires, pieces of content, or visual images.

Importantly, Stephan and his team didn't simply aim to build a digitalized version of their flawed existing process. Their ambition was to achieve the process better, faster, and cheaper—in that order. This was foundational to their approach and an important early key to gaining momentum and energy behind the change. If Kate had simply told people in other areas of the organization that they had to switch from a familiar process to a new, online platform, she would have met a lot of resistance. Instead, she framed the change as the starting point for designing better tools that gave more impactful outcomes.

Kate and Stephan also thought about how insights talent should show up differently within the creative development process and used the digitalization of insights' test-and-learn capabilities as an opportunity to elevate the role. Each stage required a mix of art and science, starting with leveraging human insights to inspire the team to build powerful creative brand platforms as a jumping off point for the creative briefing. Insights has a critical leadership role in elevating the universal human truth at the heart of the brief by ensuring it is fresh, intuitive, and contains a creatively fertile tension. As the work begins to take shape, insights need to help the team grow the idea's potential through a series of learning loops with consumers to discover what's working and what can be done to make the investment work harder.

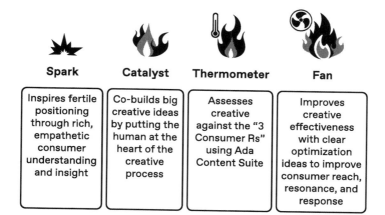

Spark	Catalyst	Thermometer	Fan
Inspires fertile positioning through rich, empathetic consumer understanding and insight	Co-builds big creative ideas by putting the human at the heart of the creative process	Assesses creative against the "3 Consumer Rs" using Ada Content Suite	Improves creative effectiveness with clear optimization ideas to improve consumer reach, resonance, and response

Role of PepsiCo's insights function in the creative process

The idea behind the model is that consumer insights are integral to the development of any ad or product innovation, from sparking ideas all the way through to optimizing the end result. A concrete example is a campaign called #CrispIN or #CrispOUT? for Walkers Crisps.[7] The penetration of the brand in the lunch occasion was in decline, though research showed that it was still the most salient, preferred, and loved snack brand in Britain. The problem was that Walkers had weak brand distinction and relevance, and didn't own the "great taste" or "high quality" space for that particular occasion.

The research aimed to generate an inspiring insight that would drive an ad campaign: an indisputable truth about consumers that revealed a need or motivation that the brand could credibly address. Insights to Inspire workshops and analysis of existing social listening data revealed a powerful insight that Walkers could use: Brits had their own "secretive" ways of enjoying crisps with sandwiches, and they loved to debate them. Out of this came an ad that discussed the pros and cons of putting crisps in a sandwich. The Ada platform was used to inspire and analyze all elements of the campaign, from storyboards to animatics to finished film. Not only were the results outstanding, but the turnaround time from commissioning a test to having tangible insights to improve projects

---

7   R Barry, "Putting the consumer at the heart of creative development", Zappi (2022), www.zappi.io/web/podcast/putting-the-consumer-at-the-heart-of-creative-development, accessed May 29, 2024

was decreased from weeks to days. The campaign won PepsiCo's Best Achievements in Marketing (BAM!) award for creative excellence that year.

This approach was especially helpful with ad testing, which was—and still is—an emotionally charged space in the marketing industry. Tight timelines and high stakes put pressure on brand managers to get ads out the door quickly. Because of this, ad testing was traditionally a rubber-stamping exercise rather than one focused on listening to consumers and using their input to improve outcomes. Kate was now able to show that her teams could get much faster feedback at lower cost using the Ada platform. Her marketing colleagues were now able to see the potential to test ideas at various stages in the production process without holding anything up. It was a stark contrast to the old way, which relied on briefing research agencies and waiting for them to present their results.

As part of creating new processes and building new tools, Stephan realized that he and his team needed to learn from other businesses with the same issues. Neither he nor Kate wanted to create something that could have benefited from outside ideas and inspiration. This led Kate to set up the Insights Alliance, a group of global organizations including Colgate-Palmolive, Mars, and Heineken. None were direct competitors, so the alliance was a safe environment for everyone to learn from one another. It became a community for advice, support, and sharing best practices. As a result, some members saw their consumer insights funding increase because they'd improved the stature of their insights functions.

Another important part of PepsiCo's new market research process resulted from broader changes within the business. During Ada's development, PepsiCo made the strategic decision to build a series of global business service (GBS) centers in Mexico and India. This was driven by the desire to create more cohesion between the different PepsiCo functions and companies around the world. The goal was to harmonize some business processes by bringing them together, so that all the people who were working on a particular process sat next to each other, working and learning as a group.

Stephan recognized the amazing opportunity this presented for Ada. By piggybacking onto this corporate-wide initiative, he could assemble a team of smart, analytically minded market research professionals in India. Their role was to provide brand managers with expert assistance and answer any questions about the data that the platform generated. Initially, the team was a modest one made up of four or five people, but it quickly grew and became integral to the efforts of the consumer insights functions in business units all over the PepsiCo world.

How to create your process

You can think of your integrated market research process as a map that plots the different journeys people will take to achieve their goals and how data will flow through the organization. To create it, there are three key stages:

1. Background preparation

2. Deciding what your process is for

3. Mapping your process

Stage One: Background preparation

Before diving into the creation of your process, you need to do some thinking up front. While it might seem that this would slow you down, getting the details right at the start results in a process that people around the business will be happy to work with. This saves time in the long run by preventing the need for extensive revisions later on. If you go ahead without this preparation, you might develop a process that's workable in some areas, but it will be by chance and not repeatable across the organization. Also, a flawed process results in a platform that's ineffective, making it challenging to gain buy-in for your new tools. It therefore makes sense to do some planning for how you intend to map it out. Following are the most important aspects to consider, in sequence, as you prepare to modernize your insights function.

Know what your business is trying to achieve

Before you do anything, review your company's strategic plans. What does the business want to achieve in the next three to five years? How does it expect to do that? If your insights transformation plan doesn't tie back to the company's plans, you'll be working in a silo and not adding true value to the business. This is the kind of thing that casts market research departments as cost centers instead of strategic assets. If you know the overall strategy, however, you'll be able to set the right success criteria and objectives for your process.

Understand how your business uses market research right now

Which business processes trigger research events? Which teams around your company use consumer insights regularly, and which don't? For those that don't, why not? A huge part of creating a new process is behavior change, so if you understand how people see and use your expertise now, you'll know where you have to do the most work to engage them. This might affect the process you put in place.

Don't skip this step. When you change processes, you change people's jobs, so it's crucial to get this right. A 360-degree understanding of your current performance will help you to optimize what's already working well and start thinking about how to onboard and implement your platform in a way that will land across all your brands, categories, and markets.

Prioritize your target countries

Familiarizing yourself with your company's strategic plans will tell you which core markets currently generate the most income, which the business is betting on (the lead markets), which it wants to activate, and which it simply needs to maintain a base in. You need to know what these markets are and in what order your new process will work across them. This will enable you to pick the right tech partner for your platform and think through how you're going to roll it out. It's a good idea to nail your core and lead markets first, then have a two-to-three-year plan to attack the rest. Don't try to boil the ocean at the first go—it will be too much of a challenge.

Take a holistic view of your brands and categories

Now it's time to take a step back and make sure you have the entire picture. Doing this is critical for two reasons. First, it helps you to build a scalable, robust sample frame so that you can consistently reach and expand your target audience. Second, reviewing your business and industry means thinking through how best to marry up all the data. For instance, how can insights about one category help you to make decisions about others?

Understand your global and local dynamics

If you work in a large, multinational organization, it's probably made up of global and local groups. Global groups focus on capabilities and key initiatives, and local groups focus on local markets, franchise management, and their own financial performance. Given that your aim is to set up a process that breaks down as many silos as possible, it's important to think through what global does, what local does, and how they'll work together—in other words, what local needs and how global can catch it in stride. This will help you to reduce logistical complications, prevent resource wastage, and maximize the benefits of your new approach.

Consider the players involved who aren't market researchers

Ad agencies tend to dislike copy testing. Brand and creative teams are comfortable with writing research briefs. Executives like the reassurance of receiving ninety-page slide decks. Understanding all of these people's needs from the start will help you to get buy-in for your process and the platform that comes out of it. More importantly, if you can configure your insights transformation in a way that inspires teams to optimize their innovation and creativity, you'll enable them to do good work.

Understand where your budget comes from and how it works

Market research departments tend to have either no budget or only part ownership of the company's research spend, with the rest coming from elsewhere in the business. Also, budgets are often split between technology and consulting, between global and local. This isn't a setup that supports a business's learning goals. If you're going to build technology, however, you'll need to pay for it. That means understanding how your budget will work in this new world. Are there opportunities for funding from outside your department? How does global versus local funding work? What about local budget allocation across your brands? Data platforms should be bought globally and give access locally, but many companies don't like to lose control in this way. While knowing this isn't fundamental to mapping out your process, it will help you to prepare for the platform that will come from it.

Bring the right people into the fold

Everything looks good on a whiteboard, but in reality, there will be a wide variety of comfort levels with this change. Knowing where there may be friction will help you to ease in the entire consumer insights team and others around the organization with different training options. While this isn't critical for your process, it will pay dividends further down the line because it's never too early to figure out who will be your piloting champions versus those who will want to join in Stage Two.

Stage Two: Deciding what your process is for

Understanding the purpose of your process is as essential as understanding the needs of its users. Ryan, one of our authors, interviewed eighty heads of market research across various businesses around the world to discover what types of research they carried out. This effort resulted in what we call the "modern-day insights stack." Where most insights departments jump from research project to research project in an ad hoc way, forward-thinking market researchers approach their insights holistically and engage in cross-project thinking. By understanding the elements of the stack, you can see how your process should answer a wide variety of business questions. Below is a nonexhaustive list of what could make up your stack:

- **Trend spotting:** Mining online conversations to identify patterns

- **Deep human understanding:** Uncovering the truths of what makes people tick

- **Pulse checking:** Asking a few short questions to get a quick read on a situation

- **Ideation:** Brainstorming ads or innovations

- **Activation insights:** Testing innovations and creative variants for insight on how to improve them to meet consumer needs

- **Shopper insights:** Analyzing consumers' retail experience

- **Experiential insights:** Understanding the overall experience you deliver

- **Market measurement:** Measuring market activity (such as sales, ad, or brand performance)

Why not reflect on your own insights stack and research cycle? Your goals should be trends insights that inform innovation testing, innovation testing that informs go-to-market testing, and in-market measurement that feeds back all the way through to the beginning of the cycle. Ask yourself whether each element of your stack is effective and enhances your business's intelligence across the board. If the answer is no in any area, build its improvement into your process.

Next, think about what questions you're regularly asked, such as "How do I make this ad better?" or "What do people think of this flavor versus that one?" Standardize a market research response to each, so that every time the question comes up you don't have to work out which methodology, vendor, or approach to use. You do the thinking once, embed it into your process, and repeat it over and over again. When you do this, your market research briefs start to disappear because decision makers can answer their own questions as they arise. What's more, data from one answer can inform all the others, so that the whole platform becomes smarter as time goes by (along with the people using it).

Trend spotting

Mine online conversations to identify patterns

Deep human understanding

Uncover the truths of what makes people "tick"

Pulse check

Ask a few short questions to get a quick read on a situation

Ideation

Brainstorm ad/innovation ideas

Activation insights zappi

Test creative & innovation ideas to get insight on how to improve them and meet consumer needs

Shopper insights

Analyze the consumer's retail shopping experience

Experiential insights

Understand the overall experience you're delivering in the market

Market measurement

Measure market activity (sales, ad-performance brand performance, etc.)

Knowledge management

Store research & insights in a central place

Consultants

Get expert help running research, interpreting results, etc

The modern marketing stack brings disparate signals into a connected system in which marketing has tools on hand that make ideas better, while insights teams curate the system and bring strategic thinking.

Pernod Ricard's approach exemplifies this. When they analyzed their insights stack, they started by defining what they would need to elevate market research above the day-to-day management of projects. They asked themselves, "What decisions do marketing teams need to make to create better ads? What's their current workflow? What metrics do they rely on? How do they work with consumer insights right now?" Only then did the business figure out which suppliers they would use to enable their process.[8]

Conversely, a major quick-service restaurant (QSR) brand that works with Zappi faced challenges when they eagerly introduced an integrated market research platform without creating a solid process first. They were in a difficult situation because they generally weren't doing enough research, and on the occasions they did, they tested new concepts too late in development and go-to-market processes, losing the opportunity to make changes. While their new platform was well received throughout the business, it didn't improve things as much as it should have. The insights team hadn't thought through the questions they wanted to answer or their success criteria, so they took a step back and did the planning.

8   Zappi, "Pernod Ricard proves it's possible to democratize insights", Zappi (2022), www.zappi.io/web/customer-stories/pernod-ricard-proves-its-possible-to-democratize-insights, accessed March 27, 2024

First, they were specific about the types of questions they wanted answers to. They became intentional about which jobs to do for each research use case, such as which specific metrics they needed. Just as importantly, they considered how those metrics would feed into their ultimate goal: to drive sales. This led them to correlate their platform to a sales outcome, which gave everyone a lot more confidence in it. Not tying platform capabilities to the business's success criteria is a common mistake. Your criteria may be growth in brand, sales, or incremental revenue; whatever it is, make sure that you're clear about it.

After the QSR brand fine-tuned their process and relaunched their platform, they saw an increase in innovation because they'd moved from a whack-a-mole approach to a systematic one. This involved training their CMO and president, along with the rest of their marketing team, on what better discipline would deliver. Eventually, the whole organization bought into the change. This enabled marketers to move from a concept-validating mindset that covered their backs to a constant learning mindset with the intent of making launches more impactful. It was a transformation in process from reactivity to proactivity, and it changed how market research was seen throughout the business.

Another mistake that many companies make is to fix just one area of their insights stack. It makes sense, of course, to focus first on the biggest problems, but they don't go on to reap the rewards that occur when all of their consumer understanding works for them beyond day-to-day projects. PepsiCo pursued a revolutionary path with their committed intention of bringing all their market research and consumer data into one integrated platform, then working backward based on priority.

Stage Three: Mapping your process

Now that you understand how your process can benefit your business, it's time to define it. This involves three main stages of activity: auditing, integrating, and democratizing.

Audit

Evaluate everything: your relationships, systems, key performance indicators (KPIs), and vendors. Using the insights stack we discussed earlier, categorize the questions you're asked, disregarding who your current vendors are for the time being.

Integrate

Build your own insights map by identifying your data layers and establishing how you create communication between them. Evaluate your strategic consulting partnerships and assess how your marketing and innovation processes must evolve to accommodate the needs of a comprehensive dataset. There are two ways to do this. One is to map the underlying data assets and find ways to provide access to those who need them. Refining your tagging methodology is key here—whether by customer journey, audience segment, market, or products—so that you can create queryable data that's easily found based on your department's needs.

The other way is to map individual people's data requirements and determine the data sources to fulfill those needs. For instance, a brand manager might require daily updates on sales and pricing data so that they can analyze the impact of price changes on sales volumes. That's not enough, though; they also want to know what *else* might have caused the changes. Sales are flat in Texas but on the rise in Florida. What happened in Florida recently? It turns out that there was a point-of-sale campaign that worked well, so could the brand manager trial it in Texas? To carry out this analysis, the brand manager doesn't only need sales and pricing data but also data about promotional campaigns. This, at its most simple level, is the process that you'd map out.

Contrast this to your current scenario, where data is probably scattered across countless locations and no one person or department knows where it sits—or even what it all is. The brand manager who wants to understand what caused a sales volume drop in Texas has to go to their consumer insights team and submit a research brief, which takes weeks to come back and involves several people's time. An intelligently designed platform, however, shrinks a week of several people's work on an issue to the time it takes the brand manager to ask a simple question: "Why did sales drop in Texas?" They receive an instant response because the platform has access to the data.

Democratize

Empower the people who need data to make decisions with self-service tools. Most insights technology has safeguards so that you can build in defaults to determine what standards people use, so there's no reason why marketers and others around the business shouldn't be able to generate their own research reports. This will seem scary for two reasons. The first is the worry that marketers will end up grading their own homework. In our experience, that doesn't happen because insights teams set clear KPIs and standards to remove the ambiguity around projects. It's insights' responsibility not just to interpret data and test results, but also to provide their broader context, whether from a need-state study or another category of work that they do.

The second (and often unvoiced) fear is that self-service makes market research roles redundant. What will you do all day if you're not project managing surveys and generating reports? Even the most confident and able consumer insights leader can struggle with change, but it offers numerous advantages. For example, freeing up time from managing projects allows you to focus on generating proactive strategic insights. You become an invaluable adviser to marketers, guiding them through complex challenges and enhancing the effectiveness of the business.

Ryan once sat in a meeting with one of Zappi's biggest customers, endlessly discussing how their new process would work. At one point, Ryan said, "I don't know why you don't just give your marketing people the data and use the time you spend on managing projects to run quarterly workshops to discuss what you've learned and how it affects business strategy."

Their head of insights, who was one of the most progressive market research people Ryan had ever met, looked across the table at him. "Ryan, then what am I going to do all day?"

"Great question," Ryan responded. "What you're going to do instead is teach your marketers how to make better ads by taking all the data inputs and feeding them proactive, strategic insights. You'll move from working tactically to strategically, and so enable marketing to use the research tools to do a much better job for their consumers."

This is a huge shift in role for a market research department. A leading telco Ryan currently works with is dealing with a lot of internal friction as their marketers clamor for access to data, but their insights team doesn't want to let go of it. Everyone is going through the process of learning that the new role of consumer insights is to set up and curate the platform, synthesize macro-level findings, and empower marketers with the right tools. Marketers own the survey brief, analysis, and resulting actions, while market researchers own the success criteria in the middle. When this business completes the implementation, they'll have transformed their research process. Rather than saying, "Call me if you want me to do a project," consumer insights professionals will say, "Marketing—you're enabled."

It's worth bearing in mind that marketers want this enablement too. They're digital natives and well versed in working with programmatic systems to make strategic decisions. By creating guardrails around the variables that require deep research expertise, marketers can leverage their existing skill sets. Selfishly, you're letting them walk with topical surveys so that you can run with large, connected datasets that answer key business problems.

In all this, let's not forget that democratic access to insights is only a catalyst for consumer centricity and business growth if your organization's culture and business capacity enable people to think through this lens. It depends on the organization you work in.

Let's look at an example. Hims & Hers offers access to treatments for a broad range of conditions across sexual health, mental health, hair loss, weight loss, and dermatology. Lauren Governale, a market research professional, joined the company two years after its founding, bringing in a valuable new function to the growing company. At first, Lauren was a team of one. With a mountain to climb, she started by discovering what data the business already had that the team wasn't aware of—and how that valuable data could help them to make better decisions. She knew the power of democratizing data, so she pooled her resources into integrating a digital platform to help track and assess the company's rapidly expanding portfolio of products and promotions.[9]

Given that she had no existing processes for generating insights, Lauren had to proactively find ways to bring consumer data to the forefront of the business's operations. She decided that she could show the impact of consumer data by applying it to a marketing exercise. This led her to help create a report called "The Future of Sex," which used insights collected across all of Hims & Hers's projects to position the brand as a leader in the category. Not only did the report resonate with consumers and help to drive new business to the company, but it was also

---

9   R Barry, "Let's talk about sex: Insights in the telehealth sector", Zappi (2022), www.zappi.io/web/podcast/lets-talk-about-sex-insights-in-the-telehealth-sector, accessed May 29, 2024

a meaningful example of how powerful the brand's marketing efforts were.

The benefits of Lauren's work driving consumer-centric decision making across her organization were two-fold: The brand saw massive growth during this time, and Lauren learned the power of democratizing data. With her small team, she was able to carve out an essential role for consumer insights in the business. Now she has more people and budget and is maintaining her agile approach to insights. This shows how, if you have buy-in from your CEO and the freedom to digitalize your market research, you can be consumer centric even if the company is still growing.

Remember, as well, that marketers will always need your help thinking through thorny problems. In addition to being a strategic adviser, you'll also be the go-to source for answers to questions like why Brand X isn't selling in Dubai or why reducing the price on Product Y hasn't yielded extra sales. Your advisory role won't be lost; in fact, it will be enhanced because you'll have more time and attention for that aspect of your job when you're not managing projects all the time.

Process mapping is the key to creating the design criteria for a platform that everyone embraces and that delivers the right data to the right people at the right time. It's something that you should take time to talk to your stakeholders about in detail: brand, sales, promotions, and any other relevant areas. Don't forget your all-important IT department, whose support will be vital (more on that in the next chapter). Your process must also meet the needs of everyone from C-suite executives to marketers in disparate regions. If it doesn't work for a brand manager in Madrid who wants to run reports every week, it won't be used effectively. If people don't use it, it won't work.

Creating a process that works

While you're mapping your process, there are three things to keep in mind:

- **Connect:** Create a single point of access for all your market research data. Only then can you gain valuable meta-learnings from your past efforts and provide insights that inform future decisions.

- **Decouple:** Separate your data procurement process from your data interpretation process. While you can still commission surveys from external survey firms, you shouldn't be using the same vendors to interpret the data for you. Instead, you should either do it yourself (when you've set up your consumer insights platform to do so) or use specialist providers. That way, you'll maximize the value of the knowledge you gain *and* retain full ownership of your data.

- **Prioritize:** Recognize that building a comprehensive process will take time, so you need to prioritize. Your process is more likely to be adopted if you go to the most critical pain point first so that you make the most impressive impact. This might mean standardizing existing processes that need overhauling or fixing one major thing that's broken.

We suggest drawing a map of your problem areas with the most friction so you can prioritize bringing in the tools that will improve them. If you remember, PepsiCo's consumer insights teams had frustration with their innovation testing tool, so they started there. When they gained the win on that, they showed that they'd both achieved better results and saved money. That paved the way for their approval to invest in more areas over time.

Some tips for making the creation of a process easier

- Take time to prepare up front so that you know the scale and scope of the task.

- Implement your process incrementally, prioritizing in a way that works for your business by brand, territory, research type, or something else.

- Don't use "live fire." It's a recipe for stress if your marketing team has a big ad campaign to launch and uses the new process for that first. Instead, test some ads that aren't under pressure and, together with all the stakeholders involved, discuss the analysis you're going to do and the decisions you're going to take. Carrying testing out in a controlled workshop environment, rather than a live one, will give comfort to everyone involved and enable you to see what's working and what's not.

- Once you've progressed to business as usual, sit down with your brand teams once a quarter and go through what you've learned about their work. Maybe ad effectiveness has gone down because you over-indexed on the celebrities used or consumers' environmental concerns weren't taken into account. You'll start to see how your job has shifted from project management to strategic input. PepsiCo's Gatorade took this approach. Marketing tested their ads once a quarter, carried out an evaluation, then used the results to put in place internal creative guardrails. For instance, they decided what points to emphasize if they were using basketball players in their ads compared to tennis players.

Creating a well-defined process is a crucial first step toward building an integrated market research platform that enables agile decision making across your organization. In the next chapter, we'll explore the creation of that platform.

The takeaways

- To create an agile market research platform, you first need to map out a process that will give you its design criteria.

- This process needs to be rooted in a set of brand and business priorities that take into account their learning goals.

- Next, you need to understand what your process is for, both in terms of its end goal and the management of the research projects within it.

- A process map enables you to see the big picture and is your first concrete step toward creating a platform that transforms your market research capability.

Action points

- **Locate and understand your company's overall strategy:** How can your process contribute toward it? What will drive competitive advantage in your category?

- **Map out how your business uses market research right now:** What is your stack? What could you improve on? What would you change?

- **Work out the budget situation:** Implementing a digital market research platform saves money in the long run, but how will your short-term finances work?

- **Create a process map:** How will your map ensure that the right data reaches the right people at the right time?

To access our FREE video series on Connected Insights, visit connectedinsights.com

FOUR

Your Platform

As you map your process, your goal is to establish the design criteria for an agile, integrated market research platform. Let's remind ourselves why this integration is important. Currently, you're dealing with disparate, disconnected datasets scattered across numerous systems, each with their unique logins, data presentation formats, and individual strengths and weaknesses. For instance, a brand manager looking to evaluate the success of their latest influencer campaign must navigate the relevant social platforms, extract the data, log in to the interface they use to access sales figures, retrieve the data, and connect the metrics from one system to the other. They must also create a slide deck to share this performance data across the organization.

This fragmentation presents significant challenges. For a start, it slows down the analysis of data because it has to be done manually, so it's not agile. Just as importantly, it doesn't tell the brand manager *why* the campaign was successful or unsuccessful because there's no way for them to integrate their findings with the market research data that would shed light on that "why." On top of that, they're unable to apply the lessons learned from previous campaigns across the business to the current one. If they want to reference the performance of this new influencer campaign at a later date, they will have to dig through messages and databases to find it.

What's more, a similar campaign might have been executed for a different brand or in another region that revealed the campaign theme to be ill-conceived. Had the marketer known that, they might have chosen a different approach from the outset. Instead, this brand manager finds themselves spending more time than they should trying to work out how to do their job rather than simply doing it well. This is why an integrated, simple-to-access platform is so valuable for agile market research.

PepsiCo's approach

From the start, Stephan and Kate envisioned creating a digital platform that would remove their reliance on market research vendors. This, they largely achieved.

While Ada is based on Zappi's technology, it isn't limited to Zappi. There are other tools in the platform's ecosystem, such as those for social listening and predictive modeling. You could think of the platform as being like a smartphone with different apps; it even allows users to communicate with one another to build community and learning.

Functionality of PepsiCo's Ada platform

A great example of how much better the digital platform works than PepsiCo's legacy ways of working is the launch of Wotsits Giants.[10] Although the new product was a big hit, the decision to release it was interesting, given the appeal of the other ideas that marketers could have chosen. The marketers started with a front-end innovation process to identify new

---

10 Zappi, "New Wotsits Giants are a huge success", Zappi (2022), www. zappi.io/web/customer-stories/walkers-launches-wotsits-giants-to-huge-success, accessed May 29, 2024

product concepts that would accelerate growth over the next three years. The result was thirty-five viable ideas, each addressing a different product angle that the brand could stretch into. Because of the flexibility of the digital platform, they could carry out early-stage concept testing of all these ideas using rough product sketches and simple descriptions.

To simplify the process, the ideas were measured on two scales:

- **Breakthrough potential:** The product's distinctiveness and perceived advantage relative to competitor offerings in the category

- **Trial potential:** Likelihood that consumers will purchase the product over a specific set of alternative options on the market

Within days, based on the combination of trial and breakthrough potential, the tool had categorized the ideas: "scale and sustain," "short-term trial," "seed and grow," "emergent," or "deprioritize." While several concepts scored well, one in particular—Wotsits Giants—scored exceptionally highly in the "short-term trial" quadrant. This indicated that the business could maximize the product's potential by getting it to market quickly.

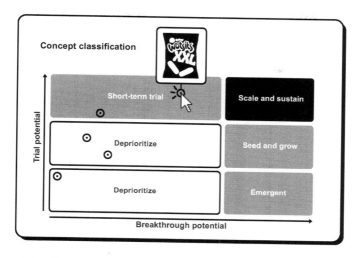

Zappi's concept classification quadrant. It charts product ideas according to their breakthrough and trial potential as a measure of distinctiveness and behavior change.

The distinction between ideas with breakthrough potential and those with incremental scale potential was something that traditional market research providers would have missed. They typically categorized the concepts as "proceed," "proceed with caution," or "stop," without providing guidance on the best approach for success or any indication of the fast timescales needed to exploit the opportunity. This resulted in a slow and costly launch. With Ada's help, however, Wotsits Giants flew off the shelves, even trending on Twitter (as it was then) without any advertising support. The whole Wotsits brand grew by 45% that year, demonstrating the halo effect of this innovation on the core product range. Given the fierce competition in the category, it was a remarkable achievement.

Ada's agility and global reach

Because Ada delivers data straight to the desks of its users, whether they be marketers or consumer insights professionals, it's far more responsive than the old method of briefing external research consultants to create PowerPoint decks. That's not its only advantage, though. Rather than sitting in silos, research data can now be cross analyzed to produce meta-learnings. (Think about it: How much easier would it be to build your next great ad concept supported by the simplicity of something akin to a Google search?)

In a company the size of PepsiCo, this has had a profound impact. If their platform contains data on 185 ads for Lay's potato chips across various countries, all featuring snacking on trains, brand managers can use insights about these ads to inform the development of the next one. For example, if 100 of these ads feature a celebrity spokesperson, brand managers can use meta-learnings to understand how these ads influence emotional response compared to the other eighty-five. Similarly, managers can compare the most effective scenarios—gaming, watching sports, a night out—via tagging taxonomy that creates comparative datasets.

Within this model, much of the learning has effectively occurred *before* the brand manager starts conceptualizing a new ad, not after. This meta-learning creates a loop in which every time an ad or new product concept is tested, it contributes to what the platform can deliver. This was impossible when teams were working manually across multiple vendors and has now become a source of PepsiCo's competitive advantage.

Another huge benefit has been the move from what Stephan calls "local for local" to "global to local." In the old days, PepsiCo carried out market research locally in individual business units by using a locally sourced research agency. That resulted in single-use data that stayed in the silo of that country or region. No other part of the business could easily access it, so much of the learning was wasted. Now, all locally generated research is fed into Ada. Given that Ada can be accessed globally, this means that teams in different countries can learn from one another, and the data is put to much more extensive use. In other words, each time a local research project is executed, the whole business gets smarter.

The creation of Ada wasn't always a smooth ride. Kate smiles when she thinks back to the early days, when she assumed that they'd have thirteen tools on the platform within five years. In reality, because it took time to gain buy-in from people, solve problems, support the change, and put in place the right governance for long-term embedment, it took them two years to perfect just one. All along, Kate recognized that being agile means constantly improving and moving forward. Her ambition is for her insights teams to test any kind of ad, even if it's on the latest social media platform. She's continually tinkering with the platform to improve it and add new capabilities, a process that will never end.

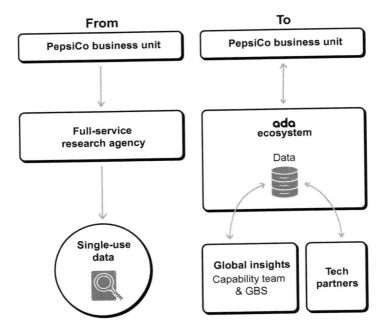

PepsiCo's move to the "global to local" Ada platform

Something that PepsiCo has found helpful all the way through the development of Ada is their collaboration with an entrepreneurial tech partner like Zappi. Most digital market research platform providers are startups, which means that in addition to giving an access point to new technology, they bring an infectious energy and ambition to established global businesses. While there have been times that PepsiCo's being a "whale" working with a "minnow" has created tensions, the partnership has pushed Kate's team to be more proactive than they would have been without the infusion of new thinking. It's made them more agile and open to change. While they acknowledge that the first two years working on Ada were hard, they now see the benefits and are having fun with it, as it fosters excitement and innovation. As inspirational entrepreneur Steve Jobs once said, "It's more fun to be a pirate than join the navy."[11]

The learning loop mentioned earlier has not only made PepsiCo's consumer insights teams more agile and produced higher-quality insights, but it's also saved them money. For a company of PepsiCo's size, moving to a systematized way of working has unlocked significant value because they save a bit each time they don't have to brief a large research agency for an individual project. Multiplied by thousands of projects, this adds up.

Systematic market research

It's worth defining what we mean by a "market research platform." Simply, it's all of the technology, data, and human resources you use to obtain the answers you need. Some people would call it a

---

11 S Todd, "The Steve Jobs speech that made Silicon Valley obsessed with pirates", *Quartz* (October 22, 2019), https://qz.com/1719898/steve-jobs-speech-that-made-silicon-valley-obsessed-with-pirates, accessed May 29, 2024

set of tools, but while tools are part of it, a platform goes beyond a collection of widgets designed for specific tasks.

Having a platform allows you to plan and process your activities, but you also need to be systematic about the way you use it. Systematic market research is a fully integrated, user-friendly approach to consumer insights that connects different technologies, vendors, and stakeholders in a way that helps you to deliver efficient and predictive insights over time. It has a number of characteristics, all of which are designed to give you remarkable benefits over and above working with a collection of disparate systems.

It's configured to your needs

In the same way that your consumers won't tolerate a one-size-fits-all product from you, you shouldn't be working with a one-size-fits-all platform. Your platform needs to allow you to set up your own sample frames and use filters to drill into specific demographics and user types. Standardizing your sample frames, which you can do once you've thought through your organization's needs, will help you to run longitudinal analysis as well. Also, you should be able to ask your own unique questions and create custom tags to describe the various aspects of your concepts, so that you can draw conclusions to compare over time.

It's important that you do this in whatever way is most meaningful for your business. For instance, think of ads designed to drive purchase consideration versus those to increase brand awareness or acquire customers from competitors. Each has a different set of KPIs, and with the personalization in your new platform, you can create robust analytics on what works for each and why. You can even establish your own weighted measure for overall effectiveness, which considers each of these factors based on their importance. If purchase consideration is most important, you can put extra stock in purchase uplift. If brand awareness is key, you can emphasize unaided brand recall and emotional intensity. Whatever matters most to your business should guide your standards for long-term usage.

Finally, you should be able to tailor your platform to the structure of your company. If, as a business, you make all decisions based on your lead market, you'll want to use your platform in a different way than if you test everything at a local level. It's important that the platform reflects the metrics and benchmarks that matter to you, and the result is that it delivers the best thinking on your terms.

It's scalable

With systematic market research, you don't answer a single question with a single test and never use those insights again. Instead, you can learn a lot more by using one platform for multiple tests and looking across those tests over time. If you want to know how to drive health-conscious consumers to your brand, for example, you can have a consistent data map that makes it easy to run analytics across all the innovation ideas your business has ever had that are relevant to your goal.

It's connected

Cast your mind back to the market research stack we talked about in the last chapter: You probably have dedicated platforms for most of those activities, such as ad and user testing. That's a lot of holistic learning you're not gaining from linking all that data together through a systematic market research platform. Your ad testing data should be talking to your concept testing data, and so on. This can bring huge benefits, not least making research a faster process.

It's always improving

When you build data over time by keeping all your results from past studies in one place, your learning is richer than if you only look at them through a series of one-off studies. Not only that, but when you approach your research in a systematic way, you set your insights people up for success. They'll spend more time connecting with others across the business and embedding market research into important decisions and less time writing research briefs or running the same studies over and over again. This means that they'll be freed up to keep up with new research trends and emerging technologies. All of this will result in cumulatively better insights, more of the time, and more quickly.

It's predictive

The whole point of market research is to predict what will happen in the real world, through a consumer lens. With systematic research, you move from validating what's already happened to predicting what will happen, because you have a way of integrating your performance data (the data that says what actually happened) into your advertising, innovation, user, brand, and packaging testing data. Over time, your platform improves and begins to help you predict real-world results more accurately. The question "Is it predictive?" should be your guiding principle when setting up your platform because once it's predictive, you and your team become critical to your organization's growth strategy.

The knowledge management center

You might be thinking, "We already have a knowledge management center in our business. Why do we need a new, integrated market research platform? Our market research reports are readily accessible through that." It's true: A knowledge management center acts as a platform that uses application programming interfaces (APIs) to give searchable access to all of the company's data. That data might be stored in PowerPoint reports, various databases, or another kind of repository.

However, unlike a digital market research platform, a knowledge management center relies on tagging to make data findable and accessible. For example, if a presentation is tagged with "strong growth," users searching for information about brands with strong growth can locate the document by entering that tag. In fact, Zappi's market research platform is one of several data repositories that knowledge management centers tap into, much like books in a library. You could think of it as being one of those books.

Many organizations have invested in knowledge management centers, including health and nutrition brand Reckitt. Reckitt adopted an external system called Stravito and branded it "The Hive." Everything goes through the Hive; it's where all Reckitt's information is housed and how they communicate within the organization. It's also allowed them to consolidate their knowledge and to transform the way that different parts of the business engage with one another.

The impact of AI on knowledge management centers

All this is about to change. Soon, AI will be able to instantaneously examine an entire company's data assets across all of its systems, harmonize the data, and make it accessible in a much more user-friendly way. This will render the knowledge management center as we know it obsolete.

How so? AI is starting to enhance or even replace the knowledge management process by becoming the user interface for data access. This will be a game changer. Just to be clear, we're not talking about the AI plugin your knowledge management center already has, but the ability for you to converse with a chat bot without navigating a dashboard or specifying criteria based on tags. That isn't even the most radical bit: Because AI has the ability to seamlessly connect with different data streams throughout your organization (including your market research data), it will soon be able to combine and compare data from diverse sources without your needing to know what tags exist. This represents a significant leap forward in data accessibility and usability.

Having a knowledge management system that stores your data could create limitless opportunities. With scalable data and consistent tagging taxonomy, you can plug these learnings into your generative AI engine of choice and create new concepts with those traits. For instance, if you're a chip brand with the goal of reaching new consumers in the United States over the next six months, you can use existing data to inspire your next idea. Your product tests in the last six months identified the highest-performing product concepts as cheese-flavored, corn-based, and spiral-shaped, so you can take those learnings and apply them to the AI engine to concept for you. Just like that, you have a product concept that's made in the consumers' image and you're ready to measure its trial and breakthrough potential.

There will be many bumps on the road to a fully AI-generated way of accessing data. The AI landscape is rapidly evolving, with multiple tools still in beta, so there will be a period of experimentation and comparison. This underscores the importance of actively participating in conversations about AI within your business. If you don't, consumer insights data is in danger of being left out of the picture. You have to be part of the program.

Where consumer insights data sits in all this

Integrating consumer insights data into the broader organizational data landscape is an important step. Unfortunately, most large companies overlook that step when designing their consumer data platform architecture, relegating consumer insights to a peripheral role. To address this, you must keep advocating for consumer insights data's importance. The most effective way to do this is to position it as "why" data. Without that, all marketers have to go on is their own interpretations of rising or falling sales over the last month or why people have stopped talking about the brand on social media. They won't have evidence on which to base their conclusions.

This is why having your own platform that seamlessly integrates with the company's data architecture is essential. This platform serves as the centralized repository for all market research data and connects to sales and other databases via APIs, maximizing your data value. Keep in mind that your data is just one piece of the larger data network within your business and that, while your IT department maps data streams across the entire organization, your market research department should do the same within the consumer insights domain.

Selecting the right market research platform vendor

You need a consumer insights platform provider that understands integration with other systems and will help you to map out your own data flows. It should also have an extensive consumer survey dataset that's easy to plug into your centralized data repository. This is usually called a customer data platform (CDP) or data management platform (DMP). While the ideal scenario is to have all your market research data within a single platform vendor, there might be instances when you want to connect to platforms that offer specialist expertise, such as pricing analysis.

Collaborating with your IT department

You may be wondering how you're going to deal with all this tech stuff, given that you're not an IT specialist. The answer is that you need to wise up to a certain extent because the consumer insights team is only part of the story of building a data architecture that enables consumer-centric decision making throughout the organization. There are also the data science and sales data teams and a host of others who must align with your platform (and yours with theirs) if your crucial "why" data is to be optimally accessible. Here's how to approach this collaboration:

- **Learn tech basics:** Familiarize yourself with fundamental tech terms and concepts, as this will enable productive discussions with IT. You'll find the "Bluffer's guide to tech terms" at the end of this book useful for that. When you ask yourself, "What's an API?" or "What does machine learning mean?" you'll find it a big help.

- **Sit down with IT:** Spend more time engaging with people in your IT department and get closer to them. Talk to them about their data strategy.

- **Frame consumer insights data:** Emphasize that consumer insights data is "why" data and highlight its pivotal role in giving explanations and contexts to decision makers. Where almost all other forms of data are "what" data ("What's the biggest brand in Venezuela?" "What sales did we make in California last week?"), market research data asks, "Why is that brand the biggest in Venezuela?" and "Why did my sales go down in California last week?" By aligning with the IT team, you can ensure that your "why" data is effectively integrated into the company's centralized data approach.

Considerations when adopting a digital market research platform

No business should have the same platform as another because each should be configured for the needs of the decision makers who use it. That said, there are some common factors to consider when implementing an agile, integrated market research platform.

Decouple data collection from data interpretation

It's essential to recognize the distinction between data collection and data interpretation. If you buy full-service research from the same vendor who generates the data, you're probably paying too much.

The two should be separate because no supplier can be equally good at both; you should see consultants as cross-data connectors and thought partners rather than tech platforms, and vice versa. Many consumer insights departments fall into the trap of asking vendors to do both tasks simultaneously. The result is either that the data doesn't work for them but the thinking does (although it's based on unreliable data) or that the data works well but the thinking that comes from it is misleading or incomplete. When you decouple data collection from interpretation, you separate the technology from the people who use it, and that's a big win.

Most businesses are decentralized, with multiple suppliers doing the same jobs in different local markets. Unilever, for instance, has outsourced the servicing of its platform to offshore service bureaus, while PepsiCo uses local talent to analyze and consult on data in the relevant territories.

Understand your regional brand or category nuances

Global businesses operate in diverse countries with distinct cultures and individual brands. While creating your platform, it's a good idea to consider these regional nuances without compromising the harmony of the data collection. It's important to be able to compare how well a brand is doing in Romania versus

Saudi Arabia versus Colombia, but at the same time, you don't want to limit innovation at a local level.

Many market research platform providers allow their clients to collect data however they want, but using different methods for data points a, b, and c means that they can't be used together. In other words, the data is great but it's only helpful for the specific task for which it was undertaken. Instead, you need a platform designed to allow multiple methods of data collection while maintaining a consistent structure for global comparison. That way, the platform remains culturally appropriate for different markets and brands and takes into account their unique competitors and challenges.

Freedom within a framework

When you create a platform that nonconsumer insights experts can use to create their own surveys and reports, giving them unlimited freedom could lead to misleading results. Nor should you restrict them unnecessarily. "Freedom within a framework" is an excellent way of balancing individual autonomy with sound decision making.

Consider your access controls and legalities

Do you want everyone in your organization to be able to see all the data in your platform? We're guessing not. Only some personnel should have unrestricted access, as certain information might be unsuitable for particular individuals or departments. You probably also have contracts with data companies that vary their charges according to the number of users, so that's another reason to limit who has access.

Implement it in an agile way

When you create an implementation plan, think of it as one clear road map managed in an agile way. That means a series of two or four weekly sprints, with clear, iterative outcomes that are tested and improved over time. Through this, you'll come up with a platform that people around the business like and approve of—one that excites and inspires them. If, instead, you disappear for a year and come back with the finished article, you'll miss a lot of adjustments that could have made it work better for them, and they may not want to adopt it.

As you envision what your platform should look like and how it must work across your business, you also need to think about who will use it: people, both you and others. That's what we'll look at in the next chapter.

The takeaways

- A digital market research platform enables you to be more agile and consumer centric.

- As the "digitalized town square" for your function, a digital market research platform allows people to connect with data, insights, and each other. It's an essential enabler for consumer insights to become a community that grows in knowledge and confidence.

- A platform offers predictive results and time-saving benefits, allowing you to take a more strategic role.

- A knowledge management center fulfills some of the requirements of an integrated market research platform but has limitations.

- Collaborating with IT is crucial for successfully implementing an agile, integrated market research platform.

Action points

- **Consider scope:** Document the scope you foresee for your business's digital market research platform.

- **Determine requirements:** Map out your platform requirements in terms of business and consumer insights priorities.

- **Work closely with IT:** Explain what you want to achieve and ask how they can help.

- **Consider subtle issues:** Discover brand and category nuances that will affect how your platform is used.

> To request a session with one of our authors for your insights team, visit connectedinsights.com

FIVE

You And Other People

You can draw up the most thorough process and create the most effective platform, but the success of both hinges on a fundamental factor: people's willingness to embrace them. Without that critical buy-in, even the best-laid plans will falter. Conversely, if people feel enthusiastic about them, you're on the way to an agile market research revolution that will embed consumer insights in the heart of your business.

Let's be real: Creating behavior change is the toughest challenge you'll face. Forget about understanding AI, tech stacks, and IT integration—they're a walk in the park in comparison. As a rule, people don't like learning new things. Think about the technology you use in your personal life and how long it took you to get used to it compared to people who are twenty years younger and grew up with it. We prefer to stick with what we know rather than go through the discomfort of grappling with something new that initially makes us feel out of our depth.

The change in how you manage people is profound. For you and your team, it means moving from:

1. Being reactive to proactive

2. Using analog systems to digital ones

3. Being order takers for projects to strategic consultants

4. Inserting yourself into the middle of the marketing process to the end

5. Focusing only on your own department to networking around the business

6. Speaking the language of market research to also speaking that of IT

7. Being a market research gatekeeper to a marketing enabler

For your colleagues in other areas of the business, it means moving from:

1. Seeing market research as a "nice to have" to embedding it into their commercial decision-making processes

2. Speaking the language of their specialty to also speaking that of consumer insights

3. Trusting the market research team they know to trusting a digital platform they don't (yet)

4. Briefing market research to manage projects to generating their own insights whenever they need them

5. Analyzing data from discrete projects to viewing all the available stats as a whole

It's quite a shift, so how do you manage these changes in a way that brings—and keeps—everyone on board? And how do you do it across a global business? This chapter is devoted to exploring exactly that. We start by looking at how PepsiCo rose to the "people" challenge. It serves as a great case study for how you might navigate this new terrain yourself. From there, we delve into your own role's evolution and what it means for you, along with that evolution's ripple effect on other people within your organization. Finally, we explore different ways that you can introduce these changes so your transformation program stands the best chance of success.

PepsiCo's approach

Whenever Stephan remembers his assumptions at the start of PepsiCo's transformation journey about what these changes would mean for people in the company, he smiles at his naivete. Back then, he assumed that if all his global consumer insights teams were unhappy with their market research tools, they'd obviously want to use something better. It was just logic. It didn't take him long, however, to realize that this notion was way off-track. What follows is the story of how he and Kate navigated the challenge of transitioning from one process and platform to another and what they learned along the way.

Let's start with the culture change they triggered by removing consumer feedback data as the trusted stoplight for projects. In PepsiCo's old way of doing things, this data tended to serve as a go/no-go decider for ads. If consumers signaled a preference for a particular creative treatment, then that was the route the brand should take. With the arrival of a digital platform that could give speedy and low-cost feedback at various stages of the ad-creation journey, however, came a much richer opportunity to inform the development of ad concepts as they went along. This was complicated and added nuance into the process, which insights professionals initially found hard to explain to marketers. There was also an onus on everyone—researchers and marketers—to stop hiding behind the data and be clearer about what they were trying to achieve. That made everyone uncomfortable for a while.

In addition, the loss of the project manager role was a challenging adjustment for many consumer insights people. Gone were the days of impressive teams of external consultants, who were adept at leveraging their firm's brand as a touchstone for quality, sweeping into the office with their forty-six-page PowerPoint decks. Instead, now there was Ada, a digital platform capable of generating data within a day or two, with consistent modeling and fast tracks to insights, which marketers were eager to explore once the survey completed. This shift left many market researchers, on the other hand, yearning for the clarity and authority of their traditional methods. Even though the old way had been suboptimal, it was at least familiar.

Not all marketers came on board easily, either. While some were enthusiastic early adopters of the platform, others had carved out long careers during which they honed their confidence in the research tools they relied on. With these old systems, it had been easy to get false positives from research, but the new platform sometimes assigned lower scores to their ad concepts than they'd received in the past. Nobody likes to be told that their baby is ugly. Reactions from marketers varied, with some curious and wanting to learn more, and others outright rejecting the new data.

Kate's teams had to manage the process gently. They had to find a way to explain that, although a marketer's baby might be ugly, the new tool could give consumer feedback in multiple ways to help make it prettier. The turning point came when marketers began to see that incorporating this feedback earlier on in the creative process led to better ratings as projects developed. Once they recognized that the insights they gained from it were measurably more useful than before, they saw it as the key to becoming more successful at their jobs.

What about those marketers who refused to realize the benefits of the new approach? Stephan adopted a three-pronged strategy for them. First and foremost, he and his team invested considerable time in handholding them through the process. Second, if necessary, Stephan also had discreet conversations with their managers, aiming to ensure back-up if required. Finally, he worked closely with the insights team in that person's market to build both the team and the marketer's confidence.

There's a nice story about the first time the platform was used on a live campaign. The UK marketing team for Walkers Crisps had signed a major US performer for a high-profile holiday ad. The Walkers insights team researched it in the traditional way before it was released, but the results were lackluster. Just as importantly, their research failed to pinpoint the reasons why consumers thought the baby was ugly. Given how pivotal the ad was and how much the brand had invested in the celebrity appearance, this was disheartening.

However, the consumer insights team had also carried out a secret test of their own using the digital platform. "Would you like to see the learning we've gained from our brand-new tool?" they asked. The marketers certainly did, and they were intrigued to discover that it produced a much more helpful diagnosis of why the ad didn't work. While the ad tested well on some metrics, such as "distinctiveness" and "overall emotion," it did poorly on others, such as "watched full ad." This translated into mediocre scores for "overall creative sales impact" and "creative brand impact."

This data enabled the Walkers team to identify the key areas in need of improvement. For instance, they pinpointed that consumers felt the central joke in the ad, which centered on the celebrity's public persona, didn't fit with the spirit of the holiday because the celebrity didn't seem to be in on the joke. While Walkers had already paid for the celebrity and couldn't change that element, they could alter the way the celebrity was portrayed to suggest a "wink" at the audience. This signaled they had a sense of humor about themselves, making the story much more humorous and light-hearted. This solution was a pivotal moment in the insights team's understanding of the benefits of the digital platform.

Over the first few months of the platform rollout, Kate came to a profound realization: She was dealing not with tool change but culture change. It became clear that she needed to focus on brand managers who were enthusiastic about the shift and work with them as a catalyst to convince others. She also discovered that the persuasive journey she was taking people on needed constant refinement. She established a routine of previewing impending changes with CMOs individually, then used their feedback to inform how information was presented in collective discussions. This process of landing buy-in from marketing leaders worked in tandem with teams seeing real results from the platform.

Another way that Stephan and Kate made people feel more comfortable with change was by setting up what they dubbed "hypercare." In part, this involved establishing a team that comprised people from their platform provider along with a newly formed unit in their India service center. The team's role was to act as a help desk for anyone who wasn't sure how to use any aspect of the platform. It became an important lifeline for the isolated consumer insights professionals scattered around PepsiCo's diverse countries and regions, as they could ask for guidance on unfamiliar tasks or advice on interpreting data.

The concentration of specialized knowledge within the India team also added an additional layer of value. While a market researcher working with a specific brand in a local market might encounter only one or two advertising campaigns a year, the India-based team touched around 1,000 ads a year across the business. This team therefore became a repository of advertising subject-matter expertise, available to any of the consumer insights business units around the world.

None of this work—training, culture change, setup of the team in India—was part of a master plan from day one. While some elements were obvious at the start, many of them evolved organically as Stephan and Kate became aware of what was needed. By the time they reached the three-year milestone in their transformative journey, one thing had become abundantly clear: Training the consumer insights teams on their new toolkit was at best only half the story. Equally important was giving them the confidence and support to thrive in their new roles. This realization led Stephan to create what he referred to as "Insights the PepsiCo Way," a new way of doing things that encouraged three behavioral shifts in how consumer insights professionals approached their work:

1. **Intentionality:** Insights professionals had to become crystal clear about who their internal clients were and what drove them. Why was a particular project so important to a brand manager? Was it related to their biggest target of the year, for instance? Had their previous two campaigns bombed? In the grander scheme of things, who was their boss and what role did they play in this?

2. **Simplicity:** With a cacophony of data points, diverse opinions, and multiple stakeholders involved in any research, it became insights professionals' responsibility to synthesize everything and distill it into the two or three insights that most mattered.

3. **Bravery:** It became part of consumer insights' job to step into the discussion, be proactive about promoting the value of market research, and stop hiding behind consultants.

To introduce Insights the PepsiCo Way, Stephan and his team carried out intense three-day global workshops on its components for a small group of "black belts." Those black belts then went on to run sessions in their respective markets and regions, and in that way the approach spread and became embedded throughout the business.

In the wake of these changes, a culture shift rippled through the consumer insights teams. They could no longer use their traditional vendors as a buffer between themselves and their internal customers. This transition was a challenge for some, but it also gave them the confidence that comes from being part of something big. A market researcher on a small team in Istanbul who might have felt isolated before could talk to Stephan's team or the India team and get whatever support they needed. Market researchers also knew that they were using the same digital platform as all the other people doing similar jobs around PepsiCo, instead of each working with their own vendors. This cohesiveness was important to Stephan, as it meant that no one was marooned on their own islands anymore.

So, what's been the outcome for the business? The digital platform is now firmly established, bolstered by a substantial team in India dedicated to support-ing insights professionals and marketers across the organization. A subset of this team focuses on help-ing people to use Ada, while the remainder work to assist business units in using the data in the most effective way and conducting meta-learning studies across markets. This means that consumer insights at PepsiCo occupies the best of both worlds: Marketers and insights professionals can generate data quickly using their digital platform, and they also have an advice team who can lend their expertise.

Further, because the platform is standardized and has removed the need for project management, it's liberated large amounts of insights professionals' time—time that they now spend on strategic work with brand managers. They no longer stand in the way of generating agile and meaningful data but add value at a higher level.

This isn't the end of the PepsiCo story. The culture change is only halfway to where it should be, so there's still more work to be done. Marketers need to deepen their understanding of the platform's nuances and learn how to harness it for the most meaningful insights. There are still many more opportunities for meta-learning, leveraging the company's scale for additional insights into what drives effectiveness. Stephan continues to find himself using a mix of incen-tives and encouragement to steer people toward using the new platform instead of reverting to the old way.

He's also mindful not to fixate on the platform itself but to emphasize what it gives people: an unrivaled way to drive creative excellence throughout the business.

All behavior change is tough, but when it's required from people who work in a field with so much ambiguity and many millions of dollars at stake, it's vital to get it right. Looking ahead, Kate envisions bringing more people with change management skills into her wider team—big thinkers who can make a compelling case for transformation. This is a good example of how implementing a new process and platform can have a knock-on effect on the kind of talent you need.

Changes to your job

Having seen how PepsiCo managed the process of change, let's look at your role. We've touched on this throughout the book, but we'll go into it in more detail here. The changes can be divided into two dimensions:

1. Changes to what you do all day

2. Changes to what kind of person you need to be

Changes to what you do all day

To illustrate the kind of changes we're talking about, let's compare the roles of a market research professional and a management consultant. Imagine watching a presentation from these professionals, one after the other. The chances are that they'll both use the same data to inform their slide decks—data that comes from the same sources and traditional survey companies. However, sadly, that's where the similarity ends. While the management consultant talks to the C-suite and commands respect as someone who can impact the direction of the business and drive growth, the market research professional typically operates at the mid-level of the organization as an information provider and has to hope that they can find a way to influence key decisions.

If you want to embrace a new way of looking at consumer insights, in which your role is no longer simply as a go-between for the business and the vendors, and no longer simply an information provider but instead to become a strategic influencer of key decisions, how could you be more like a management consultant? Instead of managing vendors and projects, could you embed an understanding of the learning from market research into the fabric of decision making around the business, much like management consultants have always been good at doing?

In other words, could you start thinking of your job as being that of a strategic adviser and a growth catalyst? This involves helping people to use market research to generate competitive advantage rather than only providing information to answer specific business questions. In a world where business decisions are increasingly agile and complex, market research must evolve into being an integral part of the process with an ongoing seat at the table rather than being brought in on a case-by-case and tactical/support role basis.

Critically, this must involve a fundamental shift in how you spend your time. One of the members of PepsiCo's GIC, Tim Warner, describes the consumer insights person's week as being made up of three types of work:

1. The "work before the work"

2. The "work"

3. The "work after the work"

Let's explain what he means by that.

The "work before the work" consists of tasks such as taking briefs from the business, translating business briefs/questions/problems into research questions, briefing different agencies, deciding what vendors and methodologies to work with, and acting as the go-between for the business and the agencies to ensure we use the most effective/predictive tools, get the most value/efficiency from our research spend, and start learning as quickly as possible.

The "work" itself is made up of all the tasks needed to execute, field, and manage the research project, and deliver learning/results to the business through managing and partnering with the chosen vendors. These buckets of work, together, can often take up more than 80% of your time, and certainly did in PepsiCo, until recently.

The remaining 20%, at best, is the "work after the work," which includes integrating and synthesizing the learning with other information sources to get to a more complete insights picture and future-forward human-centric POV, to better inform the business question. This ensures the learning is highly visible across the organization and is understood by stakeholders via powerful storytelling. It should inspire and influence for maximum impact on decision making, be monetized, partner with the business to think through all the different possible implications of the learning, and determine how we best implement and action the insights in the marketplace to strengthen the brand/business. Essentially these are things that management consultants excel at, and which drive high business value, but which research teams historically have spent very little time on, and in which they are typically less effective and impactful.

The Ada platform has enabled PepsiCo's consumer insights people to begin the process of transforming from a 40:40:20 ratio of time spent to a ratio that looks more like 10:10:80. They are increasingly spending more time on high value activities that help the business become more human centric and make stronger, faster, and better decisions, and less time on work that can be digitalized and sped up or which adds lower business value.

Another way to think of it is like this:

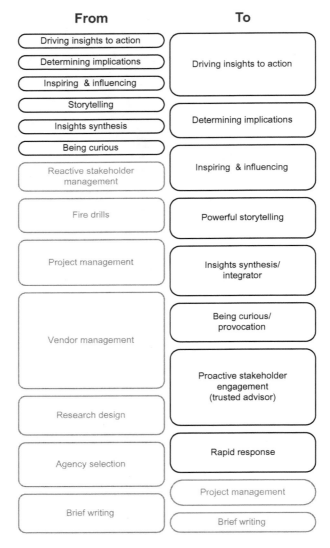

Proportion of time the average market research professional spends on different tasks

Think carefully about how much time you currently spend on vendor management, project managing tasks, and providing information, compared to really catalyzing human-centric decision making. "Being curious/Provocation," "Insightssynthesis/Integration," "Proactive stakeholder engagement (trusted adviser)," "Powerful storytelling," "Inspiring and influencing," "Partnering with the business to determine all the implications of the learning," and "Driving insights to action" probably take up a much smaller part of your day compared to acting as a go-between, selecting and managing vendors, working on methodologies, managing projects, and dealing reactively with stakeholder emergencies and fire drills. Then look at how you could and should spend your time in the new world of agile and democratized market research. You'd channel far more time and energy into generating insights (vs information) and ideas, driving visibility of insights, and embedding learning into decision making around the business, while cultivating trusted relationships with stakeholders that power human-centric growth. The burden of managing vendors and projects, working on methodologies, and dealing with emergencies and briefs would considerably reduce. Where would you prefer to spend your time? Where would you have most business impact?

This shift has already happened in the software industry, as we saw more than twenty years ago when software-as-a-service (SaaS) businesses like Salesforce burst onto the scene. They revolutionized data accessibility but also introduced their own set of challenges. In the early days, users of these cloud-based systems had to figure out how to navigate them at the same time as leveraging them for business growth—an impossible task. To alleviate the burden, a new business function known as revenue operations emerged. Almost overnight, thousands of technology solutions sprang up to support growth teams within organizations.

Similarly, in consumer insights today there are hundreds of market research tech players. This can be as overwhelming for the market research manager who's trying to choose between them as it was for the growth officer of a business in 2002. In response, some global businesses have recently acknowledged the need for a central team that's responsible for the market research insights technology stack. Their job is to understand stakeholder needs, procure software solutions to meet those needs, and then to enable the insights managers to do their jobs effectively and efficiently, with far less time spent on the "work before the work" and the "work," and increased focus on the "work after the work." This kind of development always happens to industries as they become digitalized, and it's what will increasingly happen in consumer insights. This must happen for insights to shift from go-betweens, project managers, and information providers who ultimately are dispensable, to trusted advisers, insights generators, and catalyzers of human-centric decision making, who are indispensable to the business.

Cleaning and homecare products company Clorox is an example of this. Their insights function has seconded a senior and two other insights people to a central capabilities team, and they're starting with agile learning. Whenever a marketer has a question that they're not able to answer using existing data, they use the capabilities team as a service bureau. The marketer briefs one of the team members to manage the project, while a senior domain expert in consumer insights collaborates with the marketer to ensure that they extract maximum value from the data.[12]

Clorox's example shows the feasibility of slowly evolving toward an agile and democratized market research process without having an integrated platform set up from the start. At the other end of the spectrum, PepsiCo has taken a comprehensive approach, with teams dedicated to people and platform enablement and data analysis. Even they started small and worked their way up.

---

12 R Barry, "The power of elastic thinking: Connecting insights to decision making", Zappi (2022), www.zappi.io/web/podcast/elastic-thinking-connecting-insights-to-decision-making, accessed May 29, 2024

Changes to what kind of person you need to be

The shift from project manager to strategic consultant is a huge change, moving you from reactive order taker to proactive, organization-wide adviser. What kind of person feels comfortable talking to people about how consumer data can help them to make better decisions? Someone who enjoys meeting people, feels confident with marketing processes, and is good at building connections.

In practical terms, this involves you discovering that there's a marketing strategy meeting happening on Wednesday, inviting yourself to it, and presenting the argument for consumer insights' presence at the table. How did you discover that meeting was happening in the first place? You became a networker, establishing relationships with the right people so that you're the expert they call when they're planning a product launch or strategic initiative.

It's not only consultancy roles that will evolve within market research, but also those for engineers, data analysts, and people who buy, curate, and enable technology. If you're a technical person and enjoy working with statistics and data, your role might change to one that connects data systems and shaping methodologies. Alternatively, if you have strong storytelling skills and commercial acumen, you'll probably gravitate toward consultancy. For those with both of these talents—a good business brain and technical skills—head of consumer insights might be an ideal fit.

Changes to other people's jobs

Now let's look at the ripple effect of these changes on other people around the business. It's quite a shift for others to go from thinking, "I'll ask the consumer insights team to do some research on this new ad," to thinking, "I need a new ad for this product, but before I generate any ideas, I'll use the market research data I already have to help me create some concepts. Then I'll test the concepts myself, and once the ad is out there, I'll see how it's working by looking at the data." In the latter scenario, where's the brief to the market research person? Where's the fifty-page PowerPoint deck from the consultant? These gave some comfort to the marketer, even if they were cumbersome and expensive. Now marketers are expected to replace the symbol of value that the PowerPoint presentation represented with a dashboard of data points that, while quick and easy to generate, seems a lot less substantial.

Not only that, but marketers are expected to use research data in a different way. Rather than viewing it to validate decisions that they've already made, the onus is on marketers to integrate it from the beginning of the innovation cycle—from concept creation, to consumer feedback on concepts, to market testing, and back to concept creation. For people who traditionally relied on their intuition or knowledge of the market to make decisions, it can be a challenge to bring consumer data into the center of the process. Following are some tips and real-world examples from companies that have successfully implemented this kind of change (and continue to do so; it's never a one-and-done thing).

Go with the grain

In your business, where does the tide naturally turn toward a more proactive approach to market research? Where are there already groups of technologically savvy people who have bought into the idea of digital transformation and are perhaps short of resources to commission research projects? Go there first, get some wins under your belt, and use them as case studies to convince others who are more resistant to change. Demonstrating the benefits of the new approach will make it increasingly difficult for late adopters to resist.

Colgate did this. With a diverse range of businesses around the world, they were looking to put their consumer insights function through a strategic transformation. The aim was to make their insights teams more impactful and their market research tools more predictive, as well as to create an agile culture that let people be more iterative in the way they worked. Although their head of insights ultimately intended to implement these changes throughout the organization, he started with the businesses that had the strongest appetite for them. These happened to be in regions that were most scarce in resources and were under pressure to react most quickly to their market environments.[13]

To gain buy-in, he needed to prove that the new way of generating insights was at least as predictive as the old way, if not more. For that reason, the relevant market research team ran their new tools alongside the existing ones for a while. This gave people in those regions confidence that the new platform was accurate and trustworthy. After that, the head of insights bubbled up those wins to enable global change.

Start small

A good place to start may be areas of your business with small budgets. These segments are often the most receptive to the cost-saving advantages of not relying on expensive market research organizations, leading them to be open to more innovative approaches. The larger markets, on the other hand, are probably flush with money and see less need for change.

---

13   R Barry, "How to be a global insights leader", Zappi (2022), www.zappi.io/web/podcast/how-to-be-a-global-insights-leader, accessed May 29, 2024

Find your allies

Mars offers a fantastic example of how to roll out a market research transformation by focusing on allies. The company's consumer insights teams recognized the need for more impactful decision making around the organization, especially in the area of concept testing, where they had a slow, outdated process and platform. They also knew that, though a digital research platform would bring better data for a third of the price, they had to introduce it in a way that gave it credibility.[14]

First, they brought in representatives from other companies that had embarked on similar journeys to share their experiences. This not only allowed Mars's teams to learn how those pioneers had addressed the challenges of implementing change, but also gave the project social proof. Next, they coopted champions from the marketing teams in each of Mars's businesses, positioning it as a career development opportunity. They called this the Sparks Program. Participants were entrusted with mobilizing change in their areas and became experts in embedding the new platform, actively seeking feedback from those who were new to it. For instance, they identified any dissatisfaction with the guardrails early on and acted as an informal help desk for others who were trying it for the first time.

---

14   R Barry, "Innovating for the future", Zappi (2022), www.zappi.io/
     web/podcast/innovating-for-the-future, accessed May 29, 2024

The outcome of this rollout was impressive. The company achieved an 80% reduction in concept testing costs and doubled learning, all within a year. Mars went on to integrate the platform into all their ecosystems and began the process of changing other aspects of consumer insights, such as up-leveling their talent and re-evaluating their third-party consultants. The pilot created momentum that paved the way for transformation throughout the business.

What you can take from this is that, by bringing at least one person from each brand and country inside, you can create champions for your cause. If you pick them well, they will help their colleagues focus on the freedom the platform will give them to make better and quicker decisions rather than on the pain of change.

Excite people

People rarely change their behavior unless they really want to, so you need to think about how you can motivate them to make the transition. One of the best ways of doing this is to emphasize what they can achieve after the transition. They'll have instant access to better data that will help them to make more effective decisions, which will enable them to contribute directly to their brand's bottom line. They'll also have experience using an advanced tool that the average marketer hasn't seen, giving them an advantage in their careers.

Understand people's brakes and accelerators

Part of the discovery when you start preparing your transition process should be to understand people's internal "brakes" and "accelerators." First, the brakes: These are factors that inhibit people from embracing change. Are they reluctant to use new technology? Do they prefer to do things the way they've always done? Do they think that market research is overrated?

Next, the accelerators: These are drivers that motivate people to change. Do they want to save money on market research? Would they like to differentiate themselves by working with innovative technology? Are they commercially savvy and aware of the need to work in a more agile way? You'll discover a wide variety of individual attitudes within each brand or country, but there's often an internal culture that predominates. When you know what that culture is, you'll have a good idea of how to pitch your encouragement to change.

Don't throw people in at the deep end

During the first seven months after the introduction of their new market research platform, the central consumer insights team at Pernod Ricard rode shotgun with marketers on every project.[15] They consistently

---

15   R Barry, "Democratizing insights in a decentralized organization", Zappi (2022), www.zappi.io/web/podcast/democratizing-insights-in-a-decentralized-organization, accessed March 27, 2024

checked up on how marketers felt about it and addressed their concerns and challenges until everyone was comfortable. This reassured marketers that they wouldn't be left to struggle with a new technology on their own, and it led to a faster and more positive adoption than would otherwise have been the case.[16]

Navigating the people aspect of change implementation is something that every business finds challenging, and the introduction of a digital market research platform is no exception. The rewards are great, however. By integrating an agile process into your business, you empower people with holistic and continually improving data that's available whenever they need it. Ultimately, this not only strengthens your business's competitive advantage, but it also brings you closer to putting the consumer in that notorious seat at the table.

The takeaways

- Building a new process and platform isn't just a technical challenge; it's also one of the hardest change management challenges you'll ever face.

- Two main sets of changes are involved: those to you and your colleagues in market research, and those to marketers around your business.

---

16 R Barry, "Democratizing insights in a decentralized organization", Zappi (2022), www.zappi.io/web/podcast/democratizing-insights-in-a-decentralized-organization, accessed March 27, 2024

- For you, the changes mean shifts in how you spend your time and the kind of person you need to be.

- People don't like change, so you need to introduce it in ways that encourage them to feel positive about it.

Action points

- **Calculate work time:** How long do you currently spend on the "work before the work," the "work" itself, and the "work after the work"?

- **Consider colleague involvement:** Make a list of the colleagues who you think will react positively to the change and work out how to maximize their support.

- **Consider yourself:** Do you have the qualities you'll need to become the new breed of market researcher? What personal development areas can you identify?

- **Consider pacing:** Identify the brakes and accelerators of the marketers you work with on a regular basis.

> To request a session with one of our authors for your insights team, visit connectedinsights.com

SIX

The Future

Our theme throughout this book is that there's a strong imperative for you to implement a consumer insights platform with all your data on it. This will enable you to move from order taker to business partner and make a significant contribution to your company's customer centricity. That's not the only reason to have a digital platform, critical though it is. The other is that we're entering a new world of scalable AI, which will cause tectonic shifts in consumer insights. Without a platform, you won't be able to use AI to anything like its fullest. It will be something else to learn how to use piecemeal rather than a superpower that will transform the effectiveness of your work.

AI is already changing everything. When it gets going, it's going to be as revolutionary as the birth of the internet, and by the time you read this book its capabilities will have progressed in ways that we find hard to imagine while we're writing it. If you find this unsettling, you're not alone. We talk to consumer insights professionals all the time who see the storm clouds of AI gathering on the horizon and wonder when they'll be drenched in the downpour.

In practical terms, AI will disrupt every phase of the research process: desk research, proposal writing, hypothesis creation, research design, projective exercises, concept creation, conversational surveys, synthetic respondents, analysis and summary, and knowledge management. Can you think of an area that's untouched? AI can design questionnaires and carry out projection exercises that go even further to prediction and synthetic respondents. While people like you will still need to manage these processes, they'll take significantly less time than they do now. A desk research project that would once have been a three-day job will take hours or even minutes.

How will this impact you? In their book, *The Future of the Professions: How Technology Will Transform the Work of Human Experts*, authors Richard and Daniel Susskind write, "The end of the professional era is characterized by four trends: the move from bespoke service; the bypassing of traditional gatekeepers; a shift from reactive to a proactive approach to professional work; and the more-for-less challenge."[17] Let's consider for a moment how critical these trends are to you.

First, there's the transition from bespoke service, which means that your work will shift from being a craft to a product. No longer will you spend time applying your deep expertise to individual research projects, nurturing them and adding your own intellectual value. Instead, projects will become more standardized, so you'll have to find other places to use your experience and understanding. There's also the bypassing of traditional gatekeepers, a role that you—as the commissioner of market research projects—have always had. Where will your power lie in the future? Next, there's the shift from reactivity to proactivity. You will have to step up and get involved with business decisions without waiting for people to ask for your opinion. This involves a fundamental change in the way you work and the way your colleagues perceive you. Finally, the more-for-less challenge will develop as information becomes accessible to all and its price falls dramatically. This is a continuation of a trend that's been happening in consumer insights for decades.

If you think that you have abundant data today, wait (not for long) until AI is fully on its way. The price and

---

17   D Susskind and R Susskind, *The Future of the Professions: How technology will transform the work of human experts* (Oxford University Press, updated edition 2022)

speed of knowledge generation will collapse, leading to even more insight than we have now. We call this outcome the "Four Ds":

- **Disrupt:** There'll be a continual stream of new processes and ideas taking over the old.

- **Digitalize:** All data will be systematized and analyzable via digital platforms of one kind or another.

- **Democratize:** People around the business, not just market research teams, will have direct access to data.

- **Demonetize:** Data will become far cheaper to obtain and so will the insights that come from it.

This might seem scary, but while AI will kill the researcher as we know it, that's not necessarily a bad thing. Can you see how the Four Ds reflect the themes we've been exploring? How, by digitalizing and democratizing your market research processes and systems, you'll be ideally placed to exploit the benefits of AI? In other words, when you have a digital platform, you'll be ready for it. It's up to you to find a way to make this change work for you and your businesses because, as People Director at OpenAI Diane Yoon has purportedly said, "Your job will be lost to someone who knows how to use AI before it is lost to AI."

The ability to ask open-ended questions at scale

When you think about the data that will go into your platform, it's important to remember an important distinction: The current world loves numbers but the new world of AI loves language. Back in the 1930s, an American magazine called *Literary Digest* (later to become the famous *Reader's Digest*) was a pioneer in market research.[18] Their experience with creating consumer polls led them to write a paper in which they explored the best types of questions to ask consumers: closed- or open-ended. When they looked at the data gained through each method, they discovered that the answers received from open-ended questions were far more interesting and insightful than those from predefined sets of responses. The problem was that, in those days, there was no way of codifying open-ended questions so they could be tabulated and interpreted at scale. It was impossible to turn text into computerized data.

We say "in those days," but as you're aware, this challenge of codification continued until relatively recently. Now, AI (and the new Large Language Models [LLMs], in particular) is changing everything. AI will help with the text codification process in two

---

18 D Lusinchi, "'President' Landon and the 1936 Literary Digest Poll: Were automobile and telephone owners to blame?", *Social Science History*, 36/1 (2016), 23–54, https://doi.org/10.1017/S014555320001035X, accessed May 29, 2024

ways. One is by acting as a chat interface between you and thousands of your consumers, allowing you to have interesting conversations with them, including asking follow-up questions based on their answers. In other words, you'll be able to have a unique conversation with each person rather than asking them all to complete the same questionnaire. The second way that AI will help is by machine-reading and analyzing this complex data for you, which means that interpreting conversational responses at scale will no longer be impossible.

If you use AI to focus more on open-ended questions, you can create much richer data that will enable you to get under the skin of why consumers make the decisions they do. What's more, AI can suggest what actions you should take as a result. This means that you'll want to generate more conversational data than you have before. For instance, instead of asking people which criteria are most important when buying a new laptop on a scale of 1 to 10, you'll have conversational exchanges that take into account the nuances of their preferences.

AI as a creative force

In May 2023, two big players, NVIDIA (a leader in AI computing) and advertising conglomerate WPP, came together with an interesting idea. They decided to upload all WPP's TV commercials into an "omniverse," or an AI-driven virtual world.[19] The goal was to enable creative teams to produce high-quality commercials from material they already had, without starting from scratch.

How does this relate to you? Let's say you're a car brand and you want to create an ad in which a family drives to the beach in their car. In this AI-powered world, you could create the ad by mixing elements from previous ads without shooting anything new. This would save you time and money and also allow you to focus your market research efforts on the things that you're not sure about. Maybe that's sourcing the perfect background music or getting the scenery right. This is an example of how AI will transform the ad-creation process.

Market researchers as prompt engineers

AI will sit on top of your data assets, using them to deliver models and visuals and to find patterns—like a super-smart helper for your data. Asking the right questions from AI tools will therefore become an increasingly important skill because if the prompts are wrong, the resulting AI-produced ads and concepts will be homogenous or badly targeted. This is

---

19 NVIDIA, "WPP partners with NVIDIA to build generative AI-enabled content engine for digital advertising", NVIDIA (May 28, 2023), https://nvidianews.nvidia.com/news/wpp-partners-with-nvidia-to-build-generative-ai-enabled-content-engine-for-digital-advertising, accessed March 27, 2024

where "prompt engineering," or the skill of asking AI tools the right questions so that they produce the right answers, comes in. Prompt engineering will become an important market research skill in its own right.

It makes sense that you, as a market researcher, are well placed to be a prompt engineer because you already know how to ask great questions and bring the answers to life for the business's use. There's skill in creating questions such as "How can we make money in organic foods?" or "How can we resonate with millennials?" This requires empathy and intuition, qualities that you possess in abundance.

The chair at the table

At the start of this book, we mentioned that Jeff Bezos, the founder of Amazon, was famous for leaving an empty chair at the conference table during meetings. This chair symbolized the presence of the customer, whom he considered to be the most important person in the room. As consumer insights transitions from data silos, each with its own limited access, to data that's integrated and democratically accessible, market researchers will soon be able to infuse the customer's influence into every decision-making process throughout the business. This will extend beyond the obvious functions, such as marketing and product development, to departments such as HR and supply chain management. Unlike the chair at Amazon, where people had only their imaginations to work with, the consumer insights functions will have rich, instantly available, and meaningful data that they can use to make decisions based on hard evidence. This will make market research much more pivotal to the business. Your data can be the customer's voice in the room, explaining the "why" behind decisions instead of only being included toward the end to confirm something. Your role won't merely involve testing; you'll be advising and helping to craft smart decisions across the board.

However, for that transformation to take place, your data must be integrated with other data streams. This also has implications for the guardrails you embed into your market research platform, which will become even more important. You'll want to avoid overwhelming people with too much data or allowing them to misinterpret it. If you set your platform up right, these concerns fade away as you shift from project manager to curator of data and consumer understanding.

It's a bit like going to an art exhibition. You don't expect to walk into a warehouse full of pictures stacked up against the walls but into a gallery where artworks are thoughtfully chosen and displayed, complete with explanations about the thinking behind them. This enables you to appreciate and gain meaning from them in a way that you couldn't do on your own. This is your job as a curator of data: guiding others through data so that they can understand it and utilize the right elements. Every business houses a huge amount of "what" data—sales data and clickstream volumes, for instance. The "why" data that's your domain might be smaller in volume, but it's richer in value. Your future mission is to ensure that it, like cream, rises to the top.

We'll round off this chapter by describing how the future of market research looks to Stephan at PepsiCo. For him, many potential changes come to mind, but let's start with what he thinks won't change: Market researchers' need for a fundamental understanding of what drives consumer behavior and the roles different product categories play in consumers' lives will remain constant. Even for "everyday" categories such as potato chips, breakfast oats, and soft drinks, understanding macro societal trends is important. For instance, think about the many changes and effects that working from home has brought to people's daily habits. People are buying fewer train tickets and lunches out, and if they snack, they do it at home. This has had an impact on the foods they purchase and how they consume them.

The future of consumer insights in his business also depends on specific markets, particularly whether they're dominated by the direct-to-consumer trend. Take China, for example. If you live in Shanghai, you probably do your grocery shopping online and have it delivered. That means the supermarkets know a lot about you. They know that you buy cranberry juice every week, and when the weather is hot, you buy more of it. They can use this knowledge themselves or sell to others with the aim of presenting you with personalized offers and promotional messages.

This way of interacting is different from placing a TV ad for cranberry juice and hoping that the right people see it. Yet, many of the current tools that the insights industry works with were born when TV was the dominant marketing medium. Digitalization and the resulting personalization of marketing has caused the collapse of the traditional advertising model, and this will only accelerate in the future. For instance, the notion of pretesting ads may become irrelevant because each consumer will see their "own" ad, which will be different from the ones that their family, friends, and neighbors see. This probably won't eliminate the need for market research to give input into ads that are in development, but it will be much more common for AI to create hundreds or thousands of ads for different people. Consumer insights' role will therefore be to help marketers learn from the ads that worked or didn't work and decide what to do as a result. That requires a digital platform.

Some time ago, Stephan identified three purposes for consumer insights in PepsiCo. They were to:

1. Lead the understanding of consumer demand, identifying growth opportunities

2. Raise the bar on marketing and innovation effectiveness, enabling growth

3. Fuel commercial excellence, optimizing that growth

In the future, he predicts that the second and third of these purposes will become increasingly automated; for instance, if PepsiCo creates an ad for a product, AI will check if it's the right fit for a consumer's profile in nanoseconds before it is sent to their Instagram account. The first purpose, however, he doesn't see being automated. That's because it's much more strategic. It's about understanding humanity rather than understanding individual humans. There won't be a machine that can do that anytime soon.

Regarding the automation of concept creation, ads are the first candidate that springs to mind, but there's also product innovation. In PepsiCo's categories, over 80% of all new products released onto the market don't stick.[20] That's incredibly wasteful, especially when you consider the number of options that are researched and tested and don't even make it to market. As a result, Stephan and Kate are looking at ways to automate social listening so that they can focus more on what people want in the first place. Social media is effectively a collection of millions of public diaries—an enormous online focus group—so Stephan and Kate are asking themselves what they can learn from people's conversations without having to read them manually.

---

20 NIQ, "The value of failures in the world of SMB", NielsenIQ (September 16, 2022), https://nielseniq.com/global/en/insights/education/2022/the-value-of-failures-in-the-world-of-smb/, accessed March 27, 2024

In the core aspects of marketing—ads and product innovation—Stephan sees a huge future opportunity for AI to improve their current processes. Even today, ChatGPT can come up with highly relevant innovation road maps for specific markets. Further, the results are as good as the messy process that humans carry out now with a lot of external help and that, at best, leads to a 15% success rate. He also sees, however, an equally large opportunity for consumer insights people to apply their human brains to the long-term, strategic aspects of market research so that they can steer the business in the right direction.

Finally, he predicts two big shifts in the culture of PepsiCo's consumer insights departments around the world. The first is that they'll continue moving toward a way of working that serves up data for continuous improvement rather than acting as the stoplight that decides whether something that's already been created should go ahead. They've already made significant inroads into this culture change, but future tools will be automated and driven by self-learning algorithms that don't require sending surveys to 500 customers and waiting for the answers.

The second culture shift is that the split between consumer insights and marketing will eventually disappear. At PepsiCo, as in most companies, the two disciplines are divided, but this division will dissolve when data for commercial decision making is equally in the hands of both marketers and consumer insights people. Consumer insights will cease to be the go-between. Of course, marketing won't become an exclusively analytics-driven profession, but there will be a strong need for people in marketing teams who understand data.

As ever, the job of bringing the outside world into the business through long-term, strategic thinking will still be crucial. Whether this works as a separate function, or becomes absorbed into marketing teams in which somebody is in charge of thinking through where the category is going, remains to be seen. PepsiCo could be looking at a future in which consumer insights and marketing become increasingly integrated and turn into a unified driving force behind all consumer-facing decisions.

The takeaways

- Having a digital market research platform is the first step toward taking advantage of the AI revolution. Without one, you'll be left behind.

- AI will enable you to carry out and analyze nuanced conversations with your consumers at scale.

- With rich, integrated, well-managed data and strategic interpretation, you can make market research an integral part of all the consumer-facing decisions in your business.

- While AI will take over many market research activities, the job of understanding the long-term market environment will remain with you.

To request complimentary copies of this book for your team, visit connectedinsights.com

What To Do Next

Consumer insights has to change if it's to be fit for the future, and it's a journey that you won't be able to undertake alone. Even if you hold a leadership role in market research within your organization, you still need to work with marketing, your CEO, and IT if you're to realize your vision of becoming truly consumer centric. To help you with this, we've pulled together a series of advice points based on what we've learned from companies that have been through this process. You'll not be surprised that key to them is what we can all learn from PepsiCo, a pioneering company in consumer insights that stands out as one of the only businesses to have fully implemented this new model across all their market research operations.

Know why you're doing this

If your company is like most, it sees market research as the stoplight that tells marketers whether their ad or new product is go or no-go. In this respect, it's treated as an optional stage in the marketing process. It can never represent the consumer's voice at the meeting table because it's not embedded in all the decisions being made. In fact, it slows things down rather than enabling smart actions in an agile way.

However, if you adopt the new market research blueprint we advocate in this book, a transformation unfolds:

- **Decision making becomes agile:** There are no more delays due to project setup, management, or waiting for results.

- **People are empowered:** Everyone can make smarter decisions when they have continuous and immediate access to consumer research data.

- **Your role becomes more strategic:** When you're liberated from project management activities, you can spend time giving strategic input into business decisions and applying your analytical skills to complex issues.

- **Better innovation:** You can integrate AI-powered intelligence into the fabric of business decision making, enabling creators and innovators to increase their effectiveness.

- **The whole business gets smarter over time:**
  Market research becomes more effective overall,
  as it automatically shares past insights and
  knowledge from across the organization with
  the relevant people. This ensures that every time
  market research is carried out in one area, the whole
  business benefits and the platform learns from itself.

As a reminder, when PepsiCo adopted these principles, their creative effectiveness improved by almost
one-third across all advertising, which meant less
waste and more ROI. For a business of PepsiCo's size,
that represents hundreds of millions of dollars in value
gained by investing in early, iterative testing. Imagine
the impact that this could have on your organization.

Know how it could work

These benefits should be enough to get you, and anyone you need to convince, inspired to take action.
Some of the first objections we often hear when we
talk to people about this are "It wouldn't work here,"
or "Sounds great, but not yet." Let us assure you: It
can work anywhere, and it can work right now. We've
collaborated with lean startups, massive multination-
als, and everything in between, and they've all been
amazed by the difference it's made to their commercial
performance. The only things that these businesses
had in common were a commitment to making consumer insights the driving force behind their decision

making and a willingness to give marketers access to those insights whenever they needed them.

That's not enough, though; we know that you'll need more concrete advice if you're to convince people it's possible to implement an agile market research platform in your organization. Try these suggestions:

- **Gain external validation:** Invite people from other companies that have successfully implemented this approach, even if only partially, to share their experiences with your CMO and CEO. There's nothing like a third-party recommendation to back up your own assertions.

- **Address marketers' pain points:** Talk to marketers about what frustrates them now about the market research process. When you have a list of issues, explain how they'll be resolved when you carry out your proposed changes.

- **Find a friendly partner:** Seek out a cooperative department or team within your organization, such as a particular brand or geographical region. Talk to them about what you want to achieve, and ask if they'll partner with you on your journey. There will be kudos for those involved when the changes are eventually rolled out business-wide.

- **Be clear and bold:** Be prepared to step up to the plate. It's important to be assertive and transparent when discussing your goals. Think about how you'd approach it if you were a marketer presenting a new product innovation, and you get the idea.

Know the answers to "But what about..."

Whenever there's change, there are people who worry about what it means for them: "It's just going to be more work for me when it's implemented," or "Sounds like a lot of effort to get it set up," or "How the heck am I going to do that?" Maybe you've felt like that as you've read this book—we wouldn't blame you. You need to think of ways to bring the skeptics on board. Part of this means starting with people who are most likely to buy into your plan, as we suggested above, but there are more options:

- **Learn from others:** Find out how other companies that have implemented similar systems addressed challenges and overcame obstacles. Their experiences can give you insights and solutions to apply to your own business.

- **Leverage success stories:** Once you've launched in a specific area and achieved some success, use data from those successes to support your plans. Demonstrating real-world outcomes will impress people.

- **Go gradually:** Find ways to talk about the change as you roll it out. People are usually happier to adopt a new way of working when they're exposed to it gradually than when it comes out of the blue.

- **Be proactive:** You know your company, so brainstorm a list of objections that you expect to face and come up with persuasive responses. Ideally, these should include quantifiable forecasts of the new platform's benefits and cost savings.

The most important thing

This journey is not so much about consumer insights as it is about consumer insights' ability to help your company to thrive. It's a change in perspective from seeing market research as a check-box exercise to seeing it as an agile, dynamic, and integral part of your organization's growth strategy.

You can go on this journey too, and when you have, it will be as if every meeting room in your business has that chair for the customer—an access point to consumer insights data. People can ask questions of the platform in real time when they're planning any kind of activity, from promotional campaigns to new product launches. You may not be as senior as the CMO or the CEO, but if you achieve what we know you can, you'll be the person putting that chair in the room. This will lead to smarter, quicker, and better-informed decisions all around.

We'll leave our final thoughts to Stephan from PepsiCo:

> The vast majority of the 320,000 people in our company are employed to do the crucial work of making, moving, and selling our products. Relatively speaking, it's only a handful of them whose job it is to look over the horizon and ask: "Are we doing the right things? What are we missing out there? Who's coming up with new stuff we don't know about? What do we need to be aware of that we're not?" This is critical work, and if the consumer insights function isn't brave and strategic enough to contribute to it, then who is?

Over to you.

To request a session with one of our authors for your insights team, visit connectedinsights.com

---

The Bluffer's Guide To Tech Terms

When you're talking with your IT colleagues, it can be helpful to understand the language they use and be able to speak it yourself. Here's a summary of what certain words and phrases mean, divided into terms with specific market research applications and those used more generally.

Tech terms with specific market research applications

Artificial Intelligence (AI): Machines or software that mimic human-like cognitive functions such as learning and problem solving. It's great for writing reports and conducting analysis, as well as potentially generating concepts.

Algorithm: A step-by-step procedure or formula for solving a problem or accomplishing a task in computing. Used in all traditional market research models, it's now being taken over by **machine learning**.

Application Programming Interface (API): Enables different software programs to communicate and share data with each other. You can use an API to move research data from suppliers to your main data platform.

Augmented reality: Blends digital elements with the real world, often viewed through devices like smartphones or smart glasses. There are already potential applications for shopper research.

Big data: Large and complex datasets that require advanced processing and analytics. More relevant for sales and media data right now, these sit within your **CDP** or **DMP** and can be aligned with survey data by using predictive modeling.

Blockchain: A decentralized and secure digital ledger technology often associated with cryptocurrencies such as Bitcoin. Companies are looking at this technology to allow respondents to maintain control of their data and sell it to multiple companies. We'll see if this works out!

Customer Data Platform (CDP) or Data Management Platform (DMP): A tool for centralizing and managing customer data to improve marketing and customer experiences. This is probably managed by your IT colleagues; getting closer to them and the data flows will make you more central to your organization.

Data integration: The process of combining data from different sources into a unified view or system. Researchers have always looked at multiple data sources, and having everything in one system makes that task much easier.

General Data Protection Regulation (GDPR): A European data protection law aimed at safeguarding individuals' privacy. In market research, it's important for protecting respondent-level data. Like other pieces of legislation, including similar data protection regulations in California, it continues to increase the value of survey data, which is typically highly compliant.

Large Language Model (LLM): An algorithm subset of **AI** that can recognize and generate text based on knowledge gained from massive datasets. These are the core of the new AIs and the ones writing reports in market research and generating questionnaires and desk research. The most famous one is currently ChatGPT.

Machine learning: A subset of **AI** that focuses on training machines to learn from data and make predictions or decisions. It's used by many companies and market research agencies for more accurate modeling than that offered by standard, static **algorithms**.

Software-as-a-Service (SaaS): Delivers software applications over the internet on a subscription basis. Increasingly, market research providers will look to charge clients this way, making your life easier because you won't have to financially manage each project.

Sharepoint or SharePoint: A Microsoft platform for collaboration and document management. This is a potential solution for knowledge management.

User Interface (UI): What users see and interact with on a digital device or application. Great research UIs make it easy for lots of your colleagues to use the system.

Virtual reality: Immersive, computer-generated environments that users can interact with. There's currently some testing going on, but a lack of consumers with headsets makes reliable sampling difficult.

More general tech terms

Back end: The server-side, behind-the-scenes part of a website or application.

Browser cache: Stores web page data locally on your device to speed up loading times on subsequent visits.

Bug: An error or flaw in a software program that causes it to behave unexpectedly or not as intended.

Cloud computing: The delivery of on-demand computing services, such as storage, databases, and software, over the internet.

Cloud migration: The process of moving digital assets and services from on-premises servers to a cloud infrastructure.

Content Management System (CMS): Software that helps users to create, manage, and publish digital content on websites.

Cybersecurity: Measures to protect computer systems, networks, and data from theft, damage, or unauthorized access.

DevOps: A set of practices that combine software development (Dev) and IT operations (Ops) to improve collaboration and automation in software development and delivery.

Encryption: The process of converting data into a code to prevent unauthorized access.

Firewall: A network security device that monitors and filters incoming and outgoing network traffic based on predefined security rules.

Front end: The user-facing part of a website or application.

Hacker: An individual with advanced computer skills who may use them for either ethical or malicious purposes.

Hypertext Markup Language (HTML): The standard programming language for creating web pages.

iFrame: An **HTML** Element used to embed one web page within another.

Internet of Things (IoT): The network of interconnected physical devices that can collect and exchange data.

IoT device: A physical object connected to the internet, often with sensors to collect and transmit data.

JavaScript: A widely used programming language for adding interactivity to web pages.

Machine vision: Using computers to interpret and understand visual information from the world, often through cameras and image processing.

Open source: Software that's freely available and which can be modified and distributed by anyone.

Python: A versatile and easy-to-read programming language for various applications.

Responsive design: An approach to design that ensures a website adapts and looks good on various devices and screen sizes.

Scrum: An agile project management framework used to manage and develop products.

Structured Query Language (SQL): A language used for managing and querying relational databases.

Technical debt: The cost of postponed software maintenance or code shortcuts.

User Experience (UX): The overall experience a user has when interacting with a product or system, with an emphasis on usability and satisfaction.

Virtual Private Network (VPN): A secure network connection that allows you to access the internet privately and securely.

Acknowledgments

This book owes its existence to the support and expertise of countless individuals along the journey. We extend our gratitude to all who have played a part in bringing this project to life.

To Ginny, who became the eyes, ears, and voice of this project: Your expertise and professionalism helped us condense decades of experience and thousands of hours into an insightful and thought-provoking how-to guide for the researchers of the future.

To Rachel Wright, our meticulous editor: Your keen eye and thoughtful suggestions sharpened our narrative and ensured clarity and impact.

To Rethink Press, our publisher and partner: Your support and belief in our vision have been invaluable from start to finish.

A special acknowledgment from all authors for Tim Warner: Tim, without you, this partnership simply wouldn't exist. Your desire to drive progress for our industry and your tenacity in crafting our original partnership has been inspiring and invaluable.

Special thanks

From Kate and Stephan of PepsiCo

Our sincere gratitude to the many PepsiCo Insights users who drove adoption within the business. To the members of the Global Insights Council (GIC) for their "tough love" and trust to grow this capability from idea to resource. We would also like to thank our Sector champions who helped drive adoption, including Alexia Anghelakou, Eleanor Atton, Joana Aznar, Annelies Van Baelen, Aline Baia, Frank Ben-Awurum, Graham Burgess, Ryan Crimmins, Maureen Devane, Erica Diago, Burcu Dolunay, Kevin Evans, Anastasiya Gerasyuk, Molly Imhoff, Kathy Johnson, Selin Kahraman, Asli Kokcu Peksen, Neil Macfarlane, Tim McEntaggart, Nikita Mashkov, Jon Oakeley, Mike Quintana, Mariangelica Rodriguez, Christine Rouchdy, David Schwartz, Cori Sices, Colin Strawson, Sioned Winfield, and Luis Alejandro Zarate.

To Jane Wakely, who wrote the foreword for this book: Thank you for constantly challenging us to improve and produce better work. Your partnership and collaboration help us orient ourselves around the billions of consumers we serve each day.

And finally, thank you to our insights colleagues who use these tools every day. It was your work and ideas that drove impact and inspired some of the best parts of this process. It is a pleasure to experiment alongside you and learn from you each day.

From Ryan and Steve of Zappi

Our heartfelt thanks go out to our incredible customers at Zappi. Your engagement and feedback are the catalysts that inspire us to innovate and push the boundaries of this industry every day.

We'd like to specifically thank our network of partners and champions who let us share their stories in this book:

- Lauren Governale, Hims & Hers
- Matt Cahill, McDonald's
- Pernod Ricard
- Reckitt
- Colgate-Palmolive

- Mars

- SoFi

Your collaboration and commitment have been extraordinary and will go a long way toward powering the consumer insights revolution.

Finally, we would like to thank the Zappi team—both past and present—for their hard work, intelligence, and drive along the way. Without you, none of this would be possible.

Personal thank yous

Ryan

To my wife, Gillian, and my children, Blake, Callum, and Declan: Thank you for always supporting my passion. To my parents, Liza, Ernie, Bilal, and Judy: I will never be able to relay my appreciation to each of you for having my back, even when nobody else did.

Steve

To my wife, Karen, and my children, Xander and Neve: Thank you for your unwavering support and patience throughout this journey. Between long hours and stressful days, you keep me grounded to what truly matters.

Stephan

To my wife Meike Hetsen: There is simply too much to list here. To my father, Miel Gans: Thank you for instilling in me the endless fascination for why people do what they do.

Finally, to my friend Marc de Swaan Arons: Thank you for introducing me to PepsiCo, a remarkable company where over the past five years I have enjoyed the professional challenge and freedom to transform my favorite business function in the world.

Kate

To my husband, Matt: You're the real MVP for putting up with my spontaneous and enthusiastic brainstorming sessions. Thank you for preventing me from launching my laptop out the window during setbacks!

To my daughters, Ava and Cora: Your eye-rolling skills are top-notch. May you inherit my love for innovation and drive, and perhaps one day you'll build your own groundbreaking ideas.

To my parents: Despite my best efforts, you still don't quite grasp what I do for a living. But hey, believing in me even when my business jargon baffles you? That's true parental magic.

May this book inspire you all to transform your lives—or at least your LinkedIn profiles.

And to you, the reader

Thank you for taking the time to read about our journey. Please don't let this be our last interaction! Connect with us, reach out, and don't be a stranger. Remember: No step is too small when taken in the right direction.

The Authors

Steve Phillips, cofounder and CEO of Zappi

 Having worked across four continents during his career in consumer insights, Steve specializes in the use of technology to automate and improve the market research process. Prior to founding Zappi, Steve founded Tonic Insight, Tuned In Research, and Spring Research, where he led research teams to uncover new insights into consumer behavior around the world. His work on consumer purchase journeys has won multiple awards, and he's a regular speaker on the topic at industry events. He's also a published

specialist on behavioral economics, and his work on the impact this thinking has on market research won the ESOMAR Best Paper award. In addition, he was the recipient of the Best New Thinking award at the MRS Conference, the ARF Great Minds certificate, and the UK Industries Innovation award. As chair of the MRS Sustainability Council, he's passionate about moving the world of insights onto a fully sustainable pathway. When he's not building the world's leading consumer insights platform, Steve can be found on the cricket pitch or studying history.

Ryan Barry, Global President of Zappi

Having helped to start Zappi's US business in 2014, Ryan is now the company's global president, overseeing its operations across product, go-to-market, and scale. He's worked in the consumer data business for over sixteen years and, having consulted with hundreds of brands over that time, still sees the same mistakes being made. That is why he wants to help market research teams become more consumer centric by making access to consumer opinion easier and more efficient. Ryan is an advisory board member at Michigan State University and is on the Insights Association's IDEAtor program, a fellowship program designed to encourage diversity, equity, and inclusion in market research. Outside of work, he's a family man who loves spending time with his wife and three children—either that or enjoying the great outdoors (preferably with a pair of skis).

Stephan Gans, SVP, Chief Insights and Analytics Officer at PepsiCo

 Born in The Netherlands, Stephan gained a master's degree in econometrics, then joined Unilever as a marketing trainee. After fifteen years in their personal care and foods categories, he left to help build global marketing consultancy EffectiveBrands, which was eventually sold to the consulting division of Kantar. Three years at Interbrand in New York City as Chief Strategy Officer followed before he joined PepsiCo in New York as Chief Consumer Insights Officer, where he's been for the past six years. Married with four children, he and his wife are getting used to being empty nesters now that their youngest child has left home to study abroad. His favorite hobby is rowing, which involves getting up at horrible times like 5am.

Kate Schardt, VP, Global Insights Capabilities and Partnerships at PepsiCo

As a global transformation leader with over twenty years of marketing, insights, and analytics experience at PepsiCo and Nielsen, Kate's focus is raising the bar of creative and brand excellence. She places strong emphasis on delivering better returns on media investment and brand equity and on fueling consumer-centric growth from world-class innovation. Her role is to lead the digitalization of brand, advertising, and innovation insights through implementing game-changing partnerships and technology.

About Zappi

Zappi is the only market research platform that makes brands smarter the more they use it. It helps companies grow by delivering fast, affordable, and high-quality consumer insights. Through its agile market research platform, users can make every new product and advertising campaign better than the last by embedding consumers' voices into the development process. Each new data point feeds a constant learning loop that helps inspire new ideas, optimize early-stage concepts, and validate late-stage ideas.

The result? Businesses discover more over time and build a culture of learning, not testing.

Zappi was named the Best Marketing Insights Platform at the 2023 MarTech Breakthrough Awards and one of the hottest MarTech companies by Business Insider. Their award-winning culture has been recognized by Fast Company, Comparably, Quirks, Great Place to Work, and more.

⊕ www.zappi.io

in www.linkedin.com/company/zappi

© www.instagram.com/zappi.io

✕ www.x.com/zappi_io